ISN'T SHE GREAT

Writers on Women-Led Comedies
From *9 to 5* To *Booksmart*

Edited by

Elizabeth Teets

Published by

Read Often. Read Well.

Published by Read Furiously. First Edition - Trenton, NJ.

ISBN: 978-1-960869-01-2

Essays
Anthology
Comedy
Women Writers
Cultural Criticism

For more information on *Isn't She Great* or Read Furiously, please visit readfuriously.com. For inquiries, please contact info@readfuriously.com.

Cover by Adam Wilson
Edited by Samantha Atzeni

Publisher's Note

The grammatical conventions used within these essays reflect the standards of both American English and British English. We recognize that grammar is also socially constructed and have presenteed the syntax as construction for readability purposes.

Read (v): The act of interpreting and understanding the written word.

Furiously (adv): To engage in an activity with passion and excitement.

Read Often. Read Well.
Read Furiously

"You must always have faith in people. And, most importantly, you must always have faith in yourself."

-Elle Woods, *Legally Blonde*

"You are the screen where my movies light up"
Francesca Lia Block, *Weetzie Bat*

To the Hollywood Theatre and her staff, volunteers, and ghosts. Always and Forever.

TABLE OF CONTENTS

THE WHOLE ENCHILADA

Elizabeth Teets

For the last five years (pandemic permitting) I have programmed and co-hosted my film series, *Isn't She Great*, at Portland, Oregon's historic arthouse the Hollywood Theatre. I host the series with my best friend Anthony, who when not co-hosting with me is better known as the celebrated drag clown Carla Rossi. Anthony and I started the show with one main goal, to show the direct link between beloved women centric comedy films and the women stand-up comedians working today. We lure the audience in by showing something that tickles their nostalgia bone, *Legally Blonde* or *Romy and Michele* and introduce them to one of my favorite up and coming comedians who does a short set before the film.

It has been the project I have been most proud of in my time as an artist. Not only for the opportunity I have been able to give the performers (for many it is the first time they have performed for a sold out theater), but for the connections I have made with the audience. By showing my favorite films, I have been able to connect with them in a new way; I hear the audience howl at a joke I have heard so many times I no longer recognize it and get to laugh again. I often see that the struggles and challenges the women face in the film are the exact same struggles and challenges of the audience. By seeing Elle Woods or Andy Sachs overcome, it feels like we too can carry on, maybe all we just need is to dress a little better and hold our heads up a little higher. Or maybe like Bridget Jones, we are already perfect exactly as we are.

In 2018, prior to the start of my own series I went to the Hollywood Theatre to watch a sold out screening of *9 to 5*, the 80s workplace comedy starring Lily Tomlin, Jane Fonda, and Dolly Parton. In the iconic film, exhausted by their toxic work culture, the women form a plan to get back at their sexist, egotistical, lying, hypocritical bigot of a boss. Naturally, their original plan goes horribly wrong, and a comedic adventure ensues. Throughout the wacky eighties hijinks, together with their skills, cunningness, gingham blazers, and the power of female friendship, they are able to get back at their boss and make a more pleasant and equitable workplace. And live in corporate capitalism happily ever after.

It is a movie they rarely let women make. Each actress plays a truly unique and fleshed out character, none of them have love interests that are relevant to the main plot, and no one dies or goes to prison or falls in love with someone they originally thought was an asshole. For once women are allowed to go on a journey and this time we can also bring our friends. The movie addresses sexual harassment, the unpaid extra roles women play in the workforce, and the glass ceiling in ways even movies made today shy away from.

While sitting in the theater two years after the election of Donald Trump, a few minutes before the film started the host who was showing the movie in relation to a charity came on stage. She announced to the audience that the news had just broken that the Weinstein company had filed for bankruptcy. The 389 women that filled the auditorium let out a primal scream of joy and release. At first we applauded and then together we cried. A lot had happened over the last few years, and despite who sat in the Oval Office, we were finally making progress.

Watching *9 to 5* has always been a somewhat bittersweet experience for me. It is a hilarious movie with an all-star cast. The clothing they wear is iconic and I had my queer awakening by Lily Tomlin when I saw her on screen, but the movie is disheartening simply because it is too familiar. The workplace harassment and negging is the same in the movie as it is for me today. I have worked for several versions of the women's evil boss Mr Heart. Each one slightly different, some of them Democrats and some of them Republicans, but each one still spews the same sexist shit at me. They believe there is equality in the workplace simply because I'm allowed to be there. From the boss who told me he "didn't know how to talk to me" since I didn't like the comments he made about my body. To the manager in another department who yells "woman on board" every time I step on his floor to stop his colleagues from making sexist jokes for the five minutes I might overhear. To me, my daily cup of ambition is running empty.

Watching the film continues to show us that as much as things change, things continue to stay the same, but hope is on the horizon. In February 2020 I would show the movie again at The Hollywood Theatre as part of *Isn't She Great*. I played *9 to 5* in the same auditorium, three days after Harvey Wenstien was found guilty of one count of criminal sexual assault in the first degree and one count of rape in the third degree. I celebrated with the audience on stage before the film, but this time the progress felt like more than a baby step.

When writing this essay in August of 2020, my series co-host Anthony posted three Instagram stories. The stories were photos from a Dave Chappelle show. Chappelle had brought Louis CK out on stage as a secret guest during a socially distant comedy show in Ohio. He had chosen him of all people as a special guest, during a long and grueling pandemic. People were already exhausted, and so maybe the timing was right. Because we had already screamed all our screams, the resurgence of the formerly disgraced comic barely made news. Anthony was particularly upset to see two of their idols on stage with CK and Chappelle: Michelle Wolf and Tiffany Haddish. Anthony was heartbroken that two women they saw as feminist icons would be willing to participate in what was clearly an attempted comeback of the man who masturbated in front of up-and-coming women comics and then intentionally stifled their careers. As much as I appreciated Anthony's disappointment, I was not surprised. My surprise and my rage had effectively run out. At least, this particular type of rage. As a woman comedian, I was used to my workplace being deeply unsafe and the biggest threat being my peers.

In *The First Wives Club* there is a famous line uttered by Bette Midler that was changed. Allegedly she asked Goldie Hawn's charter Elise Elliot in regard to her plastic surgery if she just had "a little bit or the whole Ivana?" This is in reference to Donald Trump's first wife, who was famous for her many cosmetic procedures. Later, the line was changed to "the whole enchilada" in order to not offend Ivana Trump. It is a line I say to myself often. Am I going to settle, or do I want the whole enchilada?

Ivana Trump makes a short cameo as herself in the last scene of *The First Wives Club*. It is particularly juicy to see Ivana in a movie that is so much about New York considering her ex-husband negotiated similar roles in many other Manhattan-based movies of the era in exchange for shooting on properties he owned. Despite this, before we showed the film, Anthony and I felt her short appearance was something that we had to prep the audience for. We were unsure how the audience would react to seeing any member of the Trump family on screen. What resulted was the best show for me, personally, of our entire run.

We screened the film right before the 2018 midterm election. Using Ivana's iconic line, "Don't get mad, get everything," we prepped the audience both for her presence and for the fight that was still to come.

"Now remember everyone: turn in your ballots because this midterm we are not going to get mad, we are going to get everything."

When Ivana appeared on screen, the audience screamed louder than they ever had before; not for Ivana herself but for what she represented in that moment: justice.

I took the energy from the audience's screams and applause when Ivana appeared at the end of the movie with me as I cast my ballot. And we did get everything. That midterm we elected more women in Congress than in the history of the nation. We elected the group of congresswomen known as "the squad" and the youngest woman ever elected to Congress, Alexandria Ocasio-Cortez.

In 2022 before the midterm elections, and after the

Supreme Court had struck down abortion rights endangering women across the United States, I tried to recapture this moment of urgency. This time I chose to show *Election*, a film I loved but had not yet felt it was time to screen. *Election* is a dark comedy starring Reese Witherspoon as Tracy Flick, an ambitious high school student in Iowa running for class president. Although the movie revolves around her campaign, she is technically the villain of the film. The protagonist is instead her teacher and student government advisor, played by Matthew Broderick as Jim McAllister, as he attempts to sabotage her campaign as he feels disgusted by Tracy's ambition and threatened by her already developed sexuality, even if that development came from an inappropriate relationship with one of Jim's fellow teachers. Although most viewers of the film sympathize with Tracy Flick more than her resentful teacher, I still wasn't ready to show a film with a female lead that was intentionally off-putting. But as I watched the women in my life prepare for a world post-Roe, I realized I didn't care anymore. That the world needed to be exposed to more women who were unlikable, sexual, and ambitious to a fault if anything was ever going to change.

Election revolves around Tracy's student body presidential campaign. Jim, hating that Tracy is running unopposed, convinces Paul, a popular football player, to run simply so Tracy had opposition. At *Election's* climax, Jim tries to hide votes and steal the election from Tracy so he doesn't have to work with her as the student body advisor, but mostly because he cannot stand the look on her face when she thinks she has won. Jim tries to give the position to Paul, his candidate who is far less qualified for the job and also seems to have no interest

6

in student government. Like many women my age, too many men have not wanted to work with me, and too many have robbed me of opportunities simply because they don't want to suffer from me having any type of success. They would rather inconvenience themselves than allow me my whole enchilada. Something that I have seen reflected over and over again in our current political system. The best part about *Election* is that although we laugh at Tracy - she is a wonderful character full of many flaws and great lines - we mostly laugh at Jim. Not *with* him - at him for being small, for being a misogynist, for being threatened by a teenage girl. Eventually Jim McAllister's plan fails and seeing Tracy on the screen triumphant gives me a glimmer of hope for the future despite the doom I still feel lingering.

I have had the privilege to spend my Saturdays with hundreds of women watching my favorite movies. *Troop Beverly Hills, Bridget Jones's Diary*, and *Working Girl*, to name a few. During each show I watch the movie in a new way, and the audience breathes life into the film, reflecting it back. I sit in the middle of the auditorium, wide awake, hearing how other women see themselves in each situation. I realize from the laughter lines that I've heard hundreds of times before are funnier than I originally thought. Every single edition of *Isn't She Great* has been magical even when the audience feels smaller than it should be or the rest of the world feels impossible. There is a specific power in a funny woman. A woman who dares to laugh at the world at herself. Even when falling flat on their face we love them and the movie they made. These movies made us strong and smart and sexy and "bend and snap" a lot. At the end of the day we remind ourselves when the world only tries to let us have a little; a money, a little confidence, a little joy, to go out and get not mad, but the whole enchilada.

*Editor's Note: The Los Angeles trial of Harvey Weinstien was ongoing during the writing and editing of this anthology.

GET YOUR OWN DAMN COFFEE

Megan J. Kaleita

After almost a decade of being an executive assistant in some iteration, I avoided movies and TV with central storylines about secretaries and assistants. I've seen enough, thanks. When I finally caved and watched *The Devil Wears Prada* (2006) I realized despite the fact that the writers spent most of the movie trying to convince me that Anne Hathaway was fat when in reality she was just wearing a baggy sweater while eating a bagel, that was the least of what pissed me off. There was a problem with the assistant/menacing boss storyline and it bugged me in a wordless way I couldn't put my finger on. After weeks of unconsciously gorging myself on movies and TV that all prominently featured a storyline with an executive assistant or secretary, I have concluded that no matter who you are or what your job title is, you are never too busy or important to not get your own damn coffee.

The David and Goliath battle of boss vs assistant is an easy-to-watch kind of movie with a handy built-in power imbalance so the audience knows who to root for almost immediately. Everyone loves an underdog. When we think of secretaries, administrative, or executive assistants, we think of a *Mad Men*-esque environment with pretty young things in tight skirts, men in suits, and an infuriating pay gap highlighted with unrealistic thigh gaps. We think of typing and filing and, yes, getting coffee. The reality of being an executive assistant for me was one where I was frequently working above my paygrade with no authority to make certain decisions while being expected to make those decisions. The entitlement of the executives I worked for was staggering. Everything felt like a professional game of The Floor is Lava. One time an executive's EpiPen wasn't covered by insurance so instead of calling their doctor or the number on the back of their insurance card like a normal unentitled individual, they had the pharmacy call me. At home. On a Saturday. I didn't even work for this person, but, boy, was everyone peeved Monday morning when I said not dying of anaphylaxis was the executive's personal responsibility, not mine.

That's the kind of conflict that makes us love *The Devil Wears Prada* because by the end of the movie Andy Sachs (played by a very not-fat Anne Hathaway) pushes back and chooses herself instead of playing Miranda Priestly's (Meryl Streep) games.

In my movie gorging, I watched things from my childhood and teens, hoping to laugh like I did when I was ten and was sadly unable to because I couldn't help but watch these movies through an adult lens. I jumped back from the aughts to the 90s and in contrast to *The Devil Wears Prada*, by the end of *Don't Tell Mom the Babysitter's Dead* (1991) we're happy Sue Ellen Crandell, played by Christina Applegate in all her 90s glory, gets the boy, saves the company from bankruptcy, and is offered her dream job. It's important to remember that both of these movies represent a specific decade and that so much has changed that Miranda Priestly and Rose Lindsey are toothless tigers compared to some of the modern SheEOs that have popped up over the years.

Don't Tell Mom the Babysitter's Dead takes place in the magical land of 1990s LA where you really can get a job by showing up and handing someone your résumé. Seventeen-year-old Sue Ellen Crandell and her four siblings are left with a babysitter while her mom goes to some rando's sheep ranch in Australia for the summer. Nothing says "1990" better than some gentle months-long parental abandonment. Sweet old Mrs. Sturak (Eda Reiss Merin), spoiler alert, is an egregious harpy who dies of natural causes less than a day into watching the children. The kids panic and anonymously drop the body at a funeral home, unaware that all the money their absentee sheep-loving mom left for food and bills is in the old woman's pocket. Sue Ellen gets a job at a garment manufacturing company, General Apparel West, by lying on her résumé. She becomes the executive assistant to CEO Rose Lindsey (Joanna Cassidy) where she's fucking up left and right but still praised for her delegation and creative thinking. It's not hard for her to make an impact because her boss seems fragile and unable to handle corporate pressure. Rose Lindsey is a badly written character who only stands up to other women and seems self-conscious and more focused on pursuing romance than doing her job. Sue Ellen is in over her head but we root for her anyway because it's the 90s, a time when blatant lies disguised as wacky hijinks were the lifeblood of most comedic plots. Also, the sheer Gen X privilege of Applegate's character declining a $37,000/year salary right out of high school in 1991 (which today would be an estimated yearly salary of $78,250) in favor of taking community college classes made me go blind with rage. Bitch, you can do both.

The Devil Wears Prada unfolds in 2006 pre-recession Manhattan, at least two years before Andy's character would have been an unpaid intern instead of an assistant. Andrea Sachs is a college grad eager to start her journalism career who gets hired as an assistant at the fictional *Runway* magazine hoping proximity to print media will give her some added clout as a writer. We've all been there, babe. There's something about writing and communicating clearly that gets the E Suite hot under the collar, so I've met a lot of writers working as executive assistants. Unlike Sue Ellen, Andy is not constantly praised, but belittled, body-shamed, insulted, and blamed for the literal weather while working under the quintessential Ice Queen, Miranda Priestly. Priestly is aloof, refuses to learn Andy's name, calls her fat, and whose mercurial displeasure carries a punitive weight for everyone around her.

As Andy tries to adjust to this post-college world that doesn't care about her major or collegiate accomplishments (same, honey, same) her friends and family get angry with her for spending too much time worrying about her job and not spending time with them. This struck a personal chord with me. I spent more time with my toxic bosses and coworkers than I did with my family and friends. I needed to find a way to survive that toxicity, sometimes that survival included emulating bad behavior or sacrificing my values in a way that would hurt people I cared about. This survival mechanism, besides getting Andy an entirely new wardrobe, costs her relationships. After some major losses she comes to the conclusion that both the job and the stress it brings are pushing her further away from the career she really wants. In

12

the end, she's happy and reconnecting with friends while she starts her writing career with a slightly better fashion sense. You go, girl.

After Andy's redemption, back at Runway, everyone bemoans her departure despite all the months they spent calling her fat and incompetent. This is a spot-on accurate depiction of what happens when an executive assistant quits. Two months after I quit an EA position to move to the West Coast and write full-time, I was still getting texts, emails, and FaceTimes on the regular asking me where the fucking AA batteries were for the keyboards in the conference room while whining about how lost everyone was without me. This baffled me because my entire career there was punctuated with frequent discussions regarding how stupid everyone thought I was. One of my coworkers even made a point to tell my husband she thought I was an idiot, knowing she was talking to my husband.

Despite *The Devil Wears Prada* and *Don't Tell Mom the Babysitter's Dead* being comedies, both movies feel a little dark around the edges aided by the fact that the power imbalance falls along the same gender lines. Here there are no swatted behinds or condescending pet names, sexual tension, or gender power struggles. They're great comedies that highlight the best, worst, and funny parts of their time periods. In the current social-selling, toxic positivity eCommerce-driven influencer world, today's iteration of the female executive is one clad in athleisure who is not just a SheEO but a thought leader who cares about your *feelings* because we are boss babe business bestie badasses and we are in this *together*. And she wants you to really be honest with her. Fictionally, both Andy and Sue Ellen don't seem too emotionally involved on a personal level with their bosses; their stress is more central to their needs. Sue Ellen is worried about repaying the company petty cash her little brother stole out of her purse (oh the 90s, a land without repercussions for white kids) and Andy is trying to make everyone in her orbit happy, not just Miranda. Their focus on their executives' happiness is driven by wanting a smooth work environment and not getting charged with a felony.

My experience as an executive assistant to women executives was unlike what I saw in movies. It highlighted a boundaryless world where my executive and I were *besties* and told each other *everything*. I worked for a woman who said my primary job function was to tell her "no" and rein her in when she went overboard with too many complicated ideas and that she just wanted someone else in control of her life, which is a painfully unprofessional thing to say to a subordinate and weird thing to want. When I followed her instructions and told her no, she would get pissed off and do the thing anyway, and eventually fired me for "holding back the business and being negative." I helped this person build a social media empire, editing videos, blogs, and interviews where she talked about how hard she worked all by herself. Excuse me, but who is writing, editing, and uploading this bullshit to Instagram for you, Laura? I'd estimate I wrote a good 70% of her content. There's invisibility that comes with being an executive assistant because the executive or CEO can't function without you but it ruins their narrative and image to give you credit, a promotion, or even a raise which is why they rely on their assistant becoming emotionally invested in the mission of the business professionally and the CEO personally. That emotional investment is multi-faceted with positive and negative parts. For me, I simultaneously wanted to impress someone I thought was my friend and make them happy while also wanting authority and resenting that this person saw me as subordinate and unequal but also couldn't cope without me. As obnoxious as the personal errands were, it was also heady and powerful to know this person needed me in a vital way. The salary was always abysmal and though I wasn't making nearly enough money, it was the emotional buy-in that made me stay. I had already put in so much emotional capital I thought the professional relationship could truly pay off. It never did.

I assumed working with women executives would be The Sisterhood of The Traveling Pantsuit, not because of what I saw on movies and TV but because my experience working for male executives was annoyingly typical: the gaslighting, tasks, and sexism were all textbook. I assumed it would be different working for women in the E Suite. And in a way, it was. The tantrums were weirder, the demands were nuanced, the mentorship was bonkers, and the emotional labor was otherworldly all while being wrapped in a cocoon of bad boundaries and oversharing. And yes, I still had to get these able-bodied adults coffee. Well, I only got one of them coffee. One woman I worked under always asked me to bring her hot water with cracked black pepper sprinkled on top, not mixed in, God help you, *never* mixed in. She'd leave the cup on her desk untouched for hours and then yell out "my pep water is cold!" so I'd rush to bring her a fresh steaming mug of sneeze juice. I always wondered if she actually liked it or if it was just a power play to make me do something stupid. That wouldn't be out of the realm of possibility and we see that a little in *The Devil Wears Prada* with picky Starbucks and steak orders. Every time you get food as an assistant is an opportunity to fuck something up. Even if the restaurant or barista made the mistake, the mark still goes on your report card.

My notes on *The Devil Wears Prada* are littered with *"this bitch can't even feed herself."* My least favorite part of being an assistant was that one of my primary duties involved helping competent adults who made triple my salary meet their basic survival needs every day. And it wasn't just food; being an executive assistant is a little like running a daycare except the kids make more money than you and can fire you. I did the typical stuff like picking up dry cleaning, but I also scheduled vet appointments for their dog's impacted anal glands, listened to parenting woes, was a therapist, cheerleader, confidant, life coach, and participated in oversharing conversations about pube removal preferences. For less than $35k a year. What can I say? I just don't have the same sparkle as Christina Applegate.

All of the emotional and personal labor bugged me, but the food fetching really got under my skin. If you are an able-bodied adult with an executive title and smartphone, you are capable of feeding yourself. I'm going to take that one step further and confidently say if you're an adult with a pointy stick and a strong stomach, you're capable of getting your own food. The classism of it all really hit me when I realized my CEO's were making a minimum of ten times my salary to have emotional breakdowns over YouTube videos while I brought them lunch and scheduled dental appointments for their kids. Regardless of job duties, I hate doing things for people if they're capable of doing it themselves, especially since my love language is acts of service, usually food-related ones. If I bring you a muffin, that's my way of saying "*I care about you deeply because your mere presence makes me aflutter and your eyes are like an autumn rainstorm just as the sun breaks through the clouds.*" It's safe to say my husband is entombed in warm sweaters, blankets, unasked-for cups of tea, and muffins. Being obligated to do that professionally and not in a consensual web-cam kind of way did not make for a healthy professional environment.

The bad personal, professional, and emotional boundaries coupled with the food fetching meant that the power dynamic would sometimes go off-kilter, especially when I was told I was responsible for reining someone in or setting boundaries that a successful professional should be able to set for herself. I became a fussy nanny, asking an adult who makes more money than I do if she ate and got a good night's rest, treating her like a surly teen, and behaving like I knew her needs better than she did. Both the women I worked for loved this level of fussing and emotional labor but would also frequently snap at me for "trying to control them" and "having bad boundaries." We see some of this in *Don't Tell Mom the Babysitter's Dead* as Rose Lindsey is an emotional mess; she's chasing a doomed workplace romance, she's insecure despite being an educated woman with corporate power, and oh my god the sexual oversharing and emotional labor she's asking of her teenage subordinate. Rose goes on a weekend trip with her slimy work boyfriend played by John Getz (who has made a career out of having resting douche face) despite the fact he just spent the afternoon trying to get Sue Ellen to run away with him. When Rose gets back to the office she asks Sue Ellen this

17

masterpiece of a question:

ROSE: Have you ever had a forty-eight-hour orgasm?

Rose Lindsey is very lucky Twitter did not exist in 1991.

Andy's level of emotional labor for Miranda Priestly isn't beyond the norm of their relationship in some instances. In Paris, she shows empathy when she finds Miranda despondent over her marriage ending, a pain Andy understands because she just broke up with her boyfriend, Nate. This is standard stuff that comes up when we have human moments at work. For me, doing emotional labor for goal-oriented women in authority tended to feel like Russian roulette: oh, you're going to trauma dump on me right before I have to tell you about a contractor who fucked up or tell you we failed a very important inspection by our governing body? Awesome. And to be controversial yet brave, Nate (Adrian Grenier) isn't a shitty boyfriend. It's well documented that you shouldn't bring your work stress home to your partner. There are entire Youtube clickholes dedicated to what a twat Adrian Grenier's character is but it's normal to be hurt by your partner bitching about work all the time and then missing your birthday because of said job. It's a garbage career that Andy doesn't want, it's making her miserable and she's spreading the misery. I've been there and the hardest lesson I learned while obsessing over a job I didn't even want was that you can fail at something you hate and it can hurt just as much, if not worse, than failing at something you're passionate about.

I saw a lot of my experiences in Andy, especially the

constant scrutiny of her body, clothes, and eating habits at work. *The Devil Wears Prada* starts with a montage of women stepping into sexy underwear and continues with a shot of Andy eating a bagel so as the audience we understand that this woman gives zero shits and cannot possibly be good at her job because of her food and fashion choices. Granny panties, carbs, and that outfit? Get it together, you frizzy bitch. Beneath all the semi-outlandish comments about her weight and appearance, as an audience, we're supposed to be a little offended for her but we're also supposed to be on Runway's side a tiny bit, too. We all love a Cinderella story, and who doesn't love a makeover?

I was always disappointed by the constant diet talk in any workspace I entered. My non-writer life was spent around smart, passionate women: medical students, psych PhDs, scientists, corporate powerhouses, and financial masterminds. With that much feminine creativity, drive, and intelligence in the room, it hurt knowing the conversation would always devolve into diet talk. As the Resident Fat Girl™, I was usually stuck in that conversation because if I so much as moved a finger the diet talk would become aimed at me. Sometimes it was subtle, others it was not. One of my bosses was adamant about fat camping me during work hours and policing what I ate, another would ask what I packed for lunch and say in a voice better suited for a Rugrats character circa 1995 "*Oh wow YUM-O*" if I brought something she thought I shouldn't be eating. That boss also said that fat women don't like the body positivity movement because our only goal in life is to become thin and we don't want our dreams taken away from us which is why fat women are more likely to bully other women for being thin than we are to be victims of fatphobia and bullying ourselves. I went home with a raging migraine that day. This type of environment made it difficult to want or accept mentorship because I could get bullshit like that from old issues of *Cosmo* and *Seventeen*. Why would I want career advice from someone who is so fantastically wrong about so many fundamental parts of my personal experience?

It was oddly cathartic rewatching these movies despite the fact that I spent the entire day after watching *The Devil Wears Prada* under a weighted blanket. I felt seen and ready to throw off the weight of once again failing at something I hadn't wanted to be doing. There's a lot happening in the world of corporate feminism and I learned a lot about where I fit as an educated woman, a fat woman, or even just a woman, and what changes we all have to advocate for in every space possible. We can keep calling each other fat or we can start changing lives and worlds. Practically, I learned a lot of very marketable skills as an assistant, skills that have translated into a relatively lucrative writing and freelancing career. But most importantly I learned, without a shadow of a doubt, that you are never too important or busy to get your own goddamn coffee.

AN UNLIKELY SHERO: HOW *JAWBREAKER* HELPED ME GET MY FIRST KISS

Samantha Mann

I'm 11 years old standing barefoot in dewy grass on the outskirts of a soccer field with my best friend Emma. We're laughing with such voracity that my vision blurs. A gust of hot summer wind smacks my stomach and bare chest. The breeze carries a mixture of fresh grass clippings and adolescent perspiration. Emma and I stand with our shirts yanked up to our necks flashing a man operating a riding lawn mower. He's ignoring us, likely mortified by our underage public display of indecency. Although my breasts at age 11 appear misshapen and unappealing, I exist wildly confident in my skin.

When I hear people describe themselves as a child, I often hear words like *playful*, *silly*, and *happy*. Some of the first words I think of when reminiscing about my childhood self are *horny*, *pervy*, and *curious*. *Odd* and *eclectic* also come to mind.

I was an elementary schooler who wore two different, but coordinating, colored socks. I kept my old baby teeth in a purple plastic treasure box and on occasion I would take them out and take a sniff. Once in second grade, I orchestrated a fake screaming match with my BFF so we could leave social studies and hang out with our guidance counselor.

Early on I found power in creating shock in my mundane, suburban world.

Despite my antics I was shy around my peers. This infliction worsened with age and the onslaught of puberty. While I was never a bonafide loser, I lived on the outskirts of the popular kids. My fear of rejection was further exacerbated in seventh grade after I was catfished by a gaggle of popular guys via AIM. Since the incident, I'd been wary of any boy who said they liked me, worried I was part of another cruel joke.

By the end of seventh grade, it seemed like everyone around me was getting their first kiss, with tongue, and I wanted in. More than anything, I wanted my first kiss to be with Christopher Sheppard, but I didn't know where to begin.

Christopher Sheppard, was a rich private school boy in our neighborhood of public-school kids. He wore exclusively Polo Ralph Lauren collared sheets, had Zac Efron shagged hair, and puppy dog brown eyes. I met Chris at a church youth group meeting that I had been invited to by a neighborhood friend. Due to the number of social groups attached to Christianity, I was in a phase of disavowing Judaism. No one batted an eye to this constant religious and social pairing in our suburb, which was located twenty minutes outside of Richmond, Virginia…the capital of the confederacy, a fact that many of my public-school teachers said with pride. Christian youth groups were where all the cool kids hung out, so it was easy to turn my back away from my lineage in order to try to hook a boyfriend. But every time I was around Chris I was unable to speak.

Isn't She Great

The summer before eighth grade I vowed to get kissed and gain some confidence. It felt like eighth grade would be a make or break kind of year. I decided to put my motion into place at our neighborhood pool. I met up with Chris and his friends, where I mostly smiled without my teeth while they talked and laughed at their own jokes. I don't remember now if I even thought they were funny. During adult swim, Chris asked me if he could buy me an ice pop and when I tried to answer, my mouth went dry and I was silent. Unable to regain any control over my vocalizations, I turned around, grabbed my belongings, and shuffled home in a soaking wet swimsuit. The summer clock was running out of time, and I had blown my chance.

Back at home, I called my BFF (*the same one from the faux screaming match) Caitlin to report my failure. She suggested a sleepover to cheer me up and assured me that boys were stupid and not to worry, that he probably hadn't even noticed. Caitlin had an older brother, which made her appear chic and worldly. She was always light years ahead of me in movies, TV shows, and music. When I arrived at her house that night, we made a list, which we hoped would be enough activities to keep us up all night. It never worked because Caitlin historically fell asleep right at the stroke of midnight. Our list that evening included: Manacala tournament, Super Mario World, Kitchen Experiments, Snacks, and to watch as many Rated R movies as we could.

*There is a saying that if you were awake last at a sleepover, you're now gay. This tracks for me, and I think has something to do with gay kids radiating social anxiety.

"I have the funniest movie to show you," Caitlin said as settled into our living room fort composed of decorative throw pillows covered in bangled beads and a lime green blow up couch. We had bowls of cheeseballs and Oreo sleeves at the ready. "It's called *Jawbreaker*, like the candy," she said as the opening credits rolled.

The movie opens in the opulent and colorful world of late 1990's California. The three most popular girls at Reagan High School are pretending to kidnap their best friend for her 18th birthday. All the girls wear skin tight dresses or micro mini skirts and six-inch heels. Everything on screen looks like candy, which I guess is the juxtaposition to the film's dark actions. When the girls arrive at the Waffle House and pop the trunk their friend is blue and stiff and dead. Courtney, played by Rose McGowan at her peak, is the ruthless group leader, who casually mentions to the group that she jammed an entire jawbreaker in Liz's throat. "You gagged her with a jawbreaker!" screams sidekick Julie which begins this sugary sweet teen drama.

The costumes are amazing, the soundtrack is insane, and the dialogue is perfect: "Ok, reality check, Liz is in the trunk of this car. And she is dead. That is a sad, fucked up thing, but you are going to walk into that school and strut your shit down the hallway like everything is peachy fucking keen," instructs Courtney as they idle in the school parking debating on whether or not to enter school. As I watched, mouth agape and eyes glued, I could feel myself coding the film in my bones. This was a feeling that happened to me, and still does, when I clicked with a piece of art and I can feel it shaping me. I knew within 20 minutes that this film would belong to the canon of films that shaped my young personality.

While I was eccentric and horny, I was also deeply insecure and the shock I felt watching Courtney Shayne strut around her school demanding what she wanted and being overtly sexual lit a bulb in my brain. For years, I carried around a sense of otherness I couldn't put my finger on, and it left me feeling socially uncomfortable even around my good friends. I felt that my impulses were sluttier than everyone around me. Sure, my friends wanted to be kissed but I wanted to see what a rock hard dick looked like up close. This was a time when Jessica Simpson and others were openly talking about saving themselves for marriage. Many of my friends were obsessed with their Christian Summer camps and wearing trendy purity rings. It wasn't easy times for a closeted lesbian, sex curious Jewish kid.

Jawbreaker showed me sexually confident women. It brought to light ideas about kink and pleasure and power in ways I had never seen done before. Courtney was never punished or ashamed for her sexuality. If anything, her games make her boyfriend more obsessed. In one scene she instructs him to lick and suck on a bright orange popsicle as if it's a dick, her dick: "suck my big stick," and then gets him to blow a popsicle while she goes down on him. Reader, I was shocked and titillated! New complex adult feelings unlocked. Sexuality is played with in the movie in a way that came off as fun, not stigmatizing.

Unlike other antiheroes of the time, Courtney didn't talk to herself or have inner dialogue that was disparaging about her body. She engaged in deeply immoral actions: a one-night stand with a man to get him accused of a rape that he didn't commit, blackmail, and killing her best friend with little to no remorse ("I killed the teen dream, deal with it") just to list a few. I'm not implying she was the moral compass of my youth, not that I was looking for one, but she did instill in me a sense of sexual power that was self-serving. Courtney also gives us one of the best and underutilized phrases from film history: *peachy fucking* keen. This is a phrase Caitlin and I would say no less than one hundred times a day at the height of our *Jawbreaker* mania.

During a time when most female protagonists were relaying messages of self-doubt, low self-esteem, and anxiety, Courtney Shayne was out here organizing murder cover-ups and playing kinky sex games with her boyfriend without breaking a sweat or worrying over other people's opinions of her. This is a woman who knows exactly how to play every situation, obviously until the end where everything unravels.

With a few weeks left of summer I decided with nothing to lose, I'd test out my CS (Courtney Shayne) alter ego. Over AIM I threw being coquettish out the window in lieu of going full blown whore. In AOL chat rooms I was having cybersex with anyone available to practice my budding sexual prowess. After a few weeks of online practice, I felt ready to put it all out there with Chris using my new alter ego.

Shimmynshke: Anna told me you thought I was hot.
ChrisDawg06: You already knew that
Shimmyshke: so what are you going to do about that
ChrisDawg06: …..
Shimmynshke: ….? I thought you'd hooked up lots of girls before…
but maybe Anna was lying. Sorry, nevermind I guess

ChrisDawg06: I have. Let's meet at the spillway
Shimmynshke: Are you sure? Its no big deal if you don't want to
ChrisDawg06: See you in 20

I brushed my teeth and dabbed on some of my mom's Clinique Happy perfume onto my wrists. I put on the only bra I owned. It was a cotton training bra that I didn't need, but I wanted him to see the straps poking out from my tank top. Chris was already at the spillway when I arrived via a teal TREK bicycle. The spillway was part of the manmade lake in our neighborhood. It was the part where the water literally spilled out. It was concrete and most days didn't have more than a few inches of water sitting in it. In the summer dried up algae pieces flaked across the bottom. This was where tweens and teens hung out to kiss, smoke menthols, and drink wine coolers. Chris was using the spillway to practice skateboard tricks. I think he was trying to impress me, but he couldn't even land an ollie. Nevertheless, I was turned on.

Sweat rolled down Chris's zit filled face. The sun beat off the pimples making them look like tiny red ants covering his cheeks and chin.

"Are you going to kiss me or what?" I shouted across the sun-soaked lawn. I'd been standing and watching politely for ten minutes already. Goose poop scattered the area like inescapable mines. Chris dodged the dookies and walked over to me. His board rolled down the cement ramp hitting a pile of stones at the bottom. Although it sounded like it cracked, he didn't look for it. He stood directly in front of me, his helmet still on and unclipped the way all the skater bois wore it. Watching the clip swing underneath his chin made me extremely horny. My insides felt like they're melting but I visualized Courtney Shayne in her silk nightie and pigtails bossing around her dumb boyfriend. I took Chris's helmet off and tossed it onto the grass.

He put his hands on my waist and stepped closer. One of his zits was so white I feared it would burst at any moment.

"Wait! We both have braces," I said, tapping my teeth worried we'd be locked together and my mom would have to drive us to the orthodontist to be forcibly unhinged.

He laughed, "Braces don't really stick together from kissing." I licked my tongue over my metal railroad tracks and hoped he was right.

"Close your eyes," he said.

I snapped them shut just as he pressed his mouth against mine. I was kissing a hot, popular boy and he was shoving his tongue into my mouth. I had done it. It felt slimy and even though I won't get my period for another four years, I felt like this was my transformation into womanhood.

"How was it?" he asked, pulling back after less than fifteen seconds.

"Peachy fucking keen," I said. I handed him back his helmet and sat on the edge on the lawn surrounded by bird shit. For the rest of the afternoon, I watched as he never landed an ollie.

FORGET ACCEPTANCE - *TROOP BEVERLY HILLS* TAUGHT ME AN APPRECIATION OF GLAMPING

Andria Kennedy

"Her recommendations for a campsite were totally unsuitable. There were no outlets. And there was dirt and bugs, and—and it rains there."

The moment Phyllis Nefler spoke those words in *Troop Beverly Hills*, nestled in the safety and comfort of a five-star bungalow, my world changed forever. Why had I endured family camping trips throughout the Nevada desert in flimsy nylon tents; stuffed into a sleeping bag on the cold hard ground? While I wailed over spiders in outhouses—outhouses!—and received parental admonishments to "toughen up," here was a woman putting her foot down and leading a charge to the Beverly Hills Hotel. I heard her declaration, and my ten-year-old heart skipped a beat.

Phyllis's indomitable character, played by Shelley Long, offered me more than the campy message of self-acceptance and a crucial warning against perming my hair. Her battle against the constant presence of dirt, skunks, and inclement weather reinforced my disdain for sleeping outdoors. In her fashionable quest for indulgence and comfort, I found my

29

answer to the plague of sleeping bags, mosquitoes, and burned marshmallows: Glamping.

Unfortunately, the Troop's hunt for all-inclusive camping resorts was 24 years ahead of its time.

"Glamping"—the luxurious combination of the outdoors with climate control, feather mattresses, and gourmet catering—didn't arrive until 2005. And most people didn't acknowledge the upgrade to traditional camping until a 2013 USA Today article titled "Posh Touches Luxe Up 'Glamping' Trend" - decades after *Troop Beverly Hills* hit theatres. That left me no recourse but to educate friends and family on the importance of pampering and indulgence when daring to venture into nature.

I did my best to make Phyllis proud—*without* the support of a Troop.

In 1989, a few months after the movie premiered, my fifth-grade class assembled for a week-long trip to Great Basin National Park in northeastern Nevada. The enormous trailer parked outside the school filled me with hopeful anticipation. (Didn't the Beverly Hills Troop hire such trucks for their camping trip?) I envisioned spacious pavilions to dominate the campsites and sturdy cots to lift our sleeping bags off the filthy ground. Monstrous coolers *must* contain tempting ingredients cooks would transform into fancy meals in the RVs accompanying our caravan. (An elementary school with the budget to hire gourmands? My imagination went full glamping mode) And, of course, we had a fleet of parental chaperones dedicated to our every need. If I needed to camp outside, at least I'd do so in style.

Reality proved as harsh a teacher as the film's evil

antagonist counselor, Velda.

There were no pavilions, just an odd assortment of tents, barely large enough for six sleeping bags squashed together *on the ground.* The bathrooms—a term I applied loosely as they lacked showers and hot water—required a hike uphill and were shared between four sites. (That math doesn't check out, even when you're talking children) Chaperones spiked hot dogs—*hot dogs!*—on sticks that looked suspiciously like the kindling they had us gather for the fire. I watched classmates render harmless marshmallows into inedible charcoal while I dreamed wistfully of the decadent fondue Phyllis prepared for her campers. Even Wilderness Girl Cookies would've been an improvement.

I protested the setup, insisting it constituted cruel and unusual punishment. My father, dressed in unfashionable jeans and his trademark blue plaid shirt (his daily uniform to this day), believed camping built "character." He also dutifully earned the nickname "Meanest Chaperone" on every field trip. A far cry from Phyllis's Troop Leader example, he dumped baked beans on my plate and told me to stop whining.

Adding insult to injury, we woke to *snow* on the ground on the third morning. Huddled in my coat and hiking boots, I lamented the lack of heaters, fleece pajamas, and electric blankets. When my classmates cried that we were getting sent home early, I was the only rational person to cheer. (Getting snowbound in a *tent* didn't top my childhood—or adult—bucket list)

I expected reasonable indulgence from my nature experiences. After all, *Troop Beverly Hills*'s Wilderness Girls weren't opposed to the outdoors. They simply wanted to stay comfortable in the process.

A desire for basic amenities—electricity, plumbing, Wi-Fi, mattresses, a mint on the pillow—led to today's booming glamping industry. People looking to hike, kayak, canoe, or relax in the most beautiful spots in the world can now do so without leaving behind a comfy bed or a stocked refrigerator.

And I've never overlooked the combination of stunning nature and basic luxury. I'm even willing to compromise on room to stretch my legs, preferably without hitting a rock or another camper in the process.

In 1990, we made a family cross-country move. The majesty of the Grand Canyon was spectacular, equaled by the charm of overfed squirrels willing to accept sunflower seeds from my hand. I basked in the sunshine, content to recognize my status as an undiscovered Disney princess. Unfortunately, I'd failed to convince my parents of the lessons from my school trip; they insisted on camping. I even tried a refresher viewing of *Troop Beverly Hills*. (Dad snored halfway through—the nerve!—and Mom interrupted with stories of her youth camping with Girl Scouts, *reinforcing* the narrative of joy in a tent) But at least they consented to the occasional cabin stayover during our country-spanning trip.

And we were at the *Grand Canyon*. The glorious expanse stretched to the horizon in both directions, with every shade of the rainbow embedded in the stone. (Who knew rock was so magical?) And at the bottom? The slimmest glimmer of the Colorado River. Definitely worth the heart-racing thrill of peeking over the rail. Even an encroaching storm failed to dampen the awe; lightning only added to the scene's power. Besides, rain isn't the worst thing to endure from the relative comfort of a campsite.

But when I pushed into the tent with my sister: *squish!*
Water. When my father and brother had set up the campsite,
they'd neglected to place the rain covers. The downpour had
saturated our sleeping bags.

Naturally, I expected my parents to call the site a loss and
find a hotel. Such an impressive natural monument was sure
to have plenty to satisfy the booming tourist industry. Visions
of luxurious cabins filled my mind as everyone squeezed into
the car.

But that dream fizzled as my parents distributed blankets
and squashed pillows. We'd be sleeping in the car—*in the car!*

Suddenly, I recalled the film's confrontation between
Phyllis and Velda at the hotel. Velda demonstrated contempt
upon finding the Troop in comfort: "You call this roughing
it?"

Phyllis remained reasonable: "One bathroom for nine
people? Yes."

I was trapped in a vehicle with five other people. No
room to stretch out, much less lay down, forced to listen
to the bear-like snoring of my father. Arms and legs waged
war for the limited space. I pulled a blanket over my head,
cursing camping, tents, and family members who felt morning
sunshine negated the need for rain covers.

As we drove away from the Canyon—soggy tents squished
into their carry bags—I counted the hotels and resorts with
"Vacancy" signs. The number of cheerful welcomes, complete
with swimming pools and miniature golf courses, rivaled the
natural majesty of Mother Nature.

"You mean in a hotel?" became my response whenever

anyone asked if I enjoyed camping. I insisted on hot running water, memory foam beds, and home-cooked meals for my outdoor experiences. People laughed, informing me that "wasn't camping." I eagerly recommended *Troop Beverly Hills* as reference material, receiving blank stares or additional laughter. That iconic part of my identity—to say nothing of glamping—didn't register for anyone else.

Camping, unfortunately, persisted.

My senior year of college in 2001, Tri-Beta hosted a weekend trip to the Everglades. Executive Board members faced mandatory attendance (so much for my pride as Secretary). I hunted for nearby hotels, offered to pay for my room, and received a lecture on participation instead. The biological honor society, so it seems, was destined to commune with biology. After a decade of avoiding camping, I faced the reality of tents and campfires again.

My last-ditch argument that animals lived near resorts fell on deaf ears.

I took Phyllis's words, "In the wilderness of life, we can never be too prepared," to heart, setting up my tent close to the bathroom and its solo electrical outlet. Friends teased there was hot water, but did that matter when the facilities lacked showers? I gritted my teeth and reminded myself the trip was one weekend; I would (probably) survive. If Phyllis could face her fears during the Wilderness Jubilee and cross a ravine on a log, I could endure a final camping experience.

Then again, Phyllis never dealt with college men. Grown men going through a mid-life crisis? Sure. (Bimbo girlfriend, sports car, trendy condo—her ex, Fred, checked all the boxes) But college men? They're a different species and *worse* in the outdoors.

Buried in the warmth of a sleeping bag designed for arctic weather—a dubious luxury—I woke to muffled shouts, frantic movements, and strange chattering in the night. I resigned myself to lost sleep and more outdoor life, climbing from the tent to confront the noise.

Armed with a flashlight and palm branches, three of my classmates clustered near the coolers, their heads pressed together in consultation.

"What are you doing?" I hissed, startling them.

"Raccoons have gotten into the food."

I stood on tiptoe to view torn boxes, ripped bags, and scattered marshmallows. Not to mention two raccoons happily dining on a stack of hot dog buns. Lifting an eyebrow, I glanced at the men in front of me. "And what are you doing?"

"Formulating a plan."

"In a hotel, *I* get to raid the minibar," I muttered. I was cold, tired, in the middle of the Everglades, and faced with the ravaging of our (adequate) meals. *Camping will* not *win this time.* I grabbed a palm branch. Waving my arms, I stomped toward the furry bandits. "All right, rascals, get out of here!"

The raccoons took in my sleep-mussed hair, shadowed eyes, and rumpled sweatshirt. No question in their eyes: I was not someone they wanted to cross. Snagging an extra bun, they disappeared into the underbrush. (Bring on my Wilderness Girl patch for animal communication)

I glared at the men, now staring in awe. "Move the food into the truck where the raccoons can't get it. Quietly. Because I'm trying to sleep."

A cold snap moved in overnight—the worst Florida saw

in decades—but at least the raccoons didn't return. The next morning, we surveyed the damage and threw out anything with scratched packaging.

I sighed with relief when I noticed the intact cookie boxes. "At least they didn't take the Thin Mints."

No way was I sacrificing a shower and cookies. When a girl is camping—not *glamping* – she needs her luxuries.

SATAN'S PANTIES: *MISS CONGENIALITY* AND FASHION AS PERFORMANCE

Aubrey Jacobowitz

I used to wear my dad's ties to high school. I'd spend a lot of time in front of his tie rack, looking at all the colors and patterns, most of which were ugly, but in a way that I loved. There's something so persistent about an ugly tie.

There was a pocket of time in the nineties, where people occasionally forgot that little girls were traditionally restricted to femininity, in order to be compliant to the capitalist nuclear family model. Tomboy aesthetic was suddenly encouraged, especially if dads wanted their daughters to be high achieving in their image.

A true child of the 90's, I would dawdle at check out lines, peering over groceries to ogle glossy magazines, dreaming of lounging in men's underwear and a white tank in a fragrance ad, or becoming the lesbian with low rise cargo pants and shaved head at the gas station. Girl power equated to backwards baseball caps and learning deeply embedded judgement of femininity.

Miss Congeniality (2000) was the perfect backdrop for my childhood, a movie starring an outcast who aligns herself with masculinity, (followed by hardcore femininity performance) as a gender-bending form of empowerment. And she was funny!

37

In the film's opening scene, Grace Hart (Sandra Bullock), our androgyn-ish hero, starts out a tomboy with a strong sense of justice, beating up a boy who was bullying someone at school. Her sweetness slips through as she helps the bullied boy recover, and in turn he rejects her for fighting his losing battle. She quickly learns that justice is not always rewarded. In fact, it is often rejected. She would do best to stay to herself and lash out at people who don't see things her way. So she punched him.

Thus begins a career of rage-infused excellence (with a smattering of masculinity coding), that continues to be overlooked by her male peers. As an adult, now a full time FBI agent, she dresses the part in a full suit and tie, she walks the walk, she sits alone at the male-infested bar and even broods alone like a man.

This seemed to be a common theme among the tomboy tropes flooding the box office in the 90's and early 00's. Girls like Christina Ricci's character in *Now and Then*, who were complex and had history, or lonely girls, like Vada from *My Girl*, who didn't fit into their environment, so naturally, gender roles didn't seem like a fit either. Finding rejection wherever you go often becomes a catalyst for rebellion, and fashion is the most visual way to push back and give yourself an aesthetic edge.

At the start of Grace's journey, as punishment for another on the job mishap where she let justice override orders, she is assigned a job as an undercover contestant in the Miss United States Pageant, in order to find intel on a potential terrorist. The FBI rigs the pageant in her favor, all she has to do is make it seem believable that she is a legitimate competitor. Despite her protests, she is informed that competing in the pageant is the only way to keep her job, which she still considers her entire identity despite feeling socially rejected.

Agent Hart is humiliated by the idea of having to participate in the extreme performance of femininity and the stereotypes that go along with it.

Cause I'm not gonna parade around in a bathing suit... by the name...Gracie Lou Freebush and all she wants is world peace?

To add insult to injury, her boss assigns "Gracie Lou Freebush" as Agent Hart's undercover identity.

Despite my affinity for ugly ties, I grew up wanting to be a star like Audrey Hepburn or anyone with their own *E! True Hollywood Story*. I spent a lot of time playing dress up as a kid. My Abuelita would often gift me garage sale silks, sexy nightgowns, and chiffon tops that fit like dresses. I would pair them with wool scarves and sunglasses, falling out of my plastic heels as I sauntered across the carpet. Anything to feel like a mature movie star.

Like Grace, I also saw clothes as a performance. My childhood was lonely just like Grace's, so I'd spend hours practicing my role as a *Serious Actress* into my double mirror closet doors, trying on different lip colors or glitter eyeshadows, acting out scenes between myself and people I knew. I was ascending my circumstances, and though my vengeance was imagined, it was comforting. Then I'd wash it all off, put on my Dodgers cap (backwards), and play plastic swords with the boy next door.

The tomboy-esque fashion of the 90's quickly gave way to my ill-fated push-up bra years, as I entered middle school in the 2000s. The aughts seemed to ask every AFAB (assigned female at birth): are you the lipgloss type or a feminist? And the counterargument, do you have worry-free sex as an empowered woman or are you a bitter masc prude?

By the time Gracie Lou came onto the scene, her attitude was familiar to tomboys everywhere. Shy but stubborn, ready to fight, and slowly becoming more and more uncomfortable growing into roles of femininity being presented to her.

Grace Hart wearing a full suit-and-tie affair made sense to me. We meet her as a tomboy, eager to connect to others but rejected for feeling entitled to equality. Her suit is her armor. It is a call to action, proof that she is ready and willing to fight for her place. In that time and place, it was gender positivity. Her pronouns? The/Job.

Being groomed into womanhood is probably similar to getting into the FBI. They recruit you, they tell you all the rules, and teach you to fight for your life. But once you're in the field, all you have left is your impulse. There's danger from all sides and everyone is a suspected enemy.

Unlike Grace at the beginning of the film, I didn't want to hate girly things in my preteen and high school years. I wanted to study them. Dita Von Teese, Kate Winslet, Julia Roberts, Whitney Houston, actresses from the 40s and 50s, or the prominent nipples on AMERICA'S NEXT TOP MODEL. The hits. It was all a fascinating possibility for the future, for an adulthood that I couldn't wait to get to.

Dressing has always been an act of hope. I thought of fashion as a key to the kind of environment I wanted to surround myself with. Gravitating toward certain silhouettes or motifs, I'd ask myself difficult life questions such as "Do I have what it takes to be an indie coffee shop girl?" and "Why do I keep stealing all my boyfriend's clothes to wear to sleep?"

I didn't have the language to understand being non-binary in the year 2000, but I acknowledged my need to be seen as having qualities of both sides of the binary, and feeling like a secret third thing. Resigned to the fate of being assigned the task of womanhood, I still appreciated femininity, but I didn't want to be a two-dimensional version.

That is why I loved watching Grace Hart morph into Gracie Lou Freebush. She too was studying femininity for the first time, through the careful guidance of her assigned pageant coach Victor Melling (Michael Caine). Throughout the film, Grace and Victor play cat and mouse through her transformation, fighting over things like bikini waxes, low calorie diets, and hair that says "Thank you very much for the Country Music Award!"

But despite the push pull we can already see a shift in Grace. She was spared the self-judgment to explore her femininity because performing femininity in a beauty pageant was her assignment. This freed her to become another version of herself without realizing it. Under all of that make-up and hair gel, she was still an agent who cared about her work. Maybe the evening gowns weren't her bag, but she didn't combust or suddenly lose her personality. And when she needs a back-up talent for the finals, she demonstrates combat moves in a frilly skirt.

Earlier generations may have subscribed to the idea of femininity as a casualty of feminism, with disparaging messaging that girls who liked shopping or had the Valley

Girl accent couldn't possibly be serious feminists. A common tomboy trend of the late 90's was to hate the color pink. But the 2000's were shaping up to be the decade where girls who liked candy-colored heels could also enjoy advocating for their basic human rights.

Miss Congeniality became a hit at such a critical time for young women who didn't want to choose between glam and grit.

For me, the climax of Grace's story comes when she confronts her fears head-on and suggests a girls' night with the other contestants, under the professional guise of gaining intel. Although at first, she assumes she would have nothing in common with the beauty queens, she dives into the belly of the beast and lets herself be vulnerable, shedding her drag in all forms to connect to these women.

While bonding at the bar after a night of pizza, fellow contestant Cheryl tells her story about being sexually harassed, and Grace's relationship to these women becomes real in a way she couldn't have imagined. Grace realizes that other women who choose differently are not the problem, but they face complex challenges of their own. No woman is two-dimensional, no matter their opinion on sparkles or nail length.

She humanized Cheryl to see her as not a victim, but a sweet, self-assured, if not naive, product of her experiences. Not only that, Cheryl's constant championing of Gracie Lou unlocks a soft part of Grace Hart that she actually likes. Beyond gender dynamics, beyond pressure to compete or succeed or seem cool, Cheryl helps Grace understand that she isn't just one thing, and maybe she'd been so stuck in one version of herself that she was unable to see the value of a different perspective. Grace had spent so much time judging these women in the same way she had been judged by her coworkers, but the encouragement they eventually have for each other is vital to her transformation.

During the interview portion of the pageant Grace is asked what she thinks of those who describe the Miss United States Pageant as anit-feminist and outdated. Grace confesses that she used to be one of them, but that she loves and respects her fellow competitors and has found the overall experience rewarding, despite falling on her face on national television.

The big surprise for me came when I found myself wanting to be more like Cheryl, whose naivety causes most of the contestants to activate their flight mode. When we first meet Cheryl, Miss Rhode Island, she recognizes Grace as Miss New Jersey, and eagerly exclaims that she's memorized the names and pictures of each contestant. Over eager to a fault, she recognizes Grace not by her photo, but her lack of one, since the FBI did not submit a pageant headshot for Gracie Lou. The other contestants discount Cherly as a push-over, or lacking a sense of self because she chooses to see the best in her competitors, and attempts to create community in the form of non-fat hot chocolate.

But beyond her natural gifts, I was also taken by Cheryl's need to break free from perfection when she feels empowered to take control of her life and commit her one bad girl move: stealing a pair of red satin panties. "*My mom called them Satan's*

Panties!"

Her conviction in her sense of self, yearning to be a certain person, the kind of person who can wear red panties, compelled her to shed her good girl 'tude. She realized, as well, there could be many parts to her.

In many ways, my desire for the perfect expression of self through fashion was summed up by Cheryl. All the outside influences that brought me to where I was: in childhood it was *Now and Then, Harriet the Spy, My Girl.* As a tween, I wanted to look fresh and sporty like Britney Spears, despite running a 15 minute mile in PE. Then later, I was into whatever Natalie Portman was doing at the time.

Cheryl's panty confession is also a turning point for Grace, who has taken such a defensive position on building herself up that she forgot pleasure and indulgence And Cheryl's guilt around stealing a pair of underwear alone made it clear she was not a suspect of, well, terrorism. She was a person with flaws but no explosives to speak of.

Cheryl's admission bonded her with Grace. She was able to get real with another woman, begin to flourish socially, and found pertinent information to help find the real terrorist. All in a day's work.

Until this point, Grace ping-pongs between performing gender with her colleagues and her fellow pageant contestants as a way to connect and deflect. When she becomes more emotionally stripped down, how she dresses is determined by how she shows up for herself every day, and that's what informs her connections in return. It's through these connections with her peers that she's able to gain intel on the pageant director and her suspiciously unfashionable son, who have a suspicious and violent past. When the FBI is certain they found their suspect elsewhere, they insist that the Miss United States Pageant is cleared of any terrorist threat. But Grace's newfound self-assuredness, along with her belief in her fellow contestants, compels her to fight to stay and protect them from potential risk. Her superior gives her the choice to move on to her next assignment or lose her job. Grace chooses to stay in the pageant, but this time she is no longer Agent Hart.

Right before the winner is announced, Grace discovers that the crown itself is the explosive and tackles Cheryl to save her. The crown explodes mid-air after Grace chucks it away from the crowd, and the pageant director and her son are arrested for an attempted terrorist attack, proving Grace's instincts were correct. She is recognized for her efforts by both the FBI, who reinstate her as an agent, and her pageant peers, who award her with the title of Miss Congeniality. She broke all the rules because she had the confidence to back herself up, and it paid off exponentially.

At the end of her assignment, as Agent Hart exits the pageant in light but visible make-up, she sums up the experience of falling into womanhood reminiscing that she will miss the heels because it did a lot for her posture, and her new awareness for her breasts.

The idea here is, she is no longer performing. She walks in tandem with Gracie Lou Freebush.

These days I'm all about a pair of trousers with a band tee or a slutty top, maybe a button-down in a partially clashing color, boots (heel optional) and oversized silver jewelry. I still love kerchiefs and vintage brooches and long elegant gloves for a special occasion, and I'm always looking for key components that will interest me and push the envelope. Texture, confusing shapes, color blocking, or anything that looks like it would be worn by a Romanian library assistant. Sometimes when I hate an item or pattern I feel inclined to prove myself wrong by wearing it. I still have a soft spot for ugly.

Each season is a new chance to evolve myself as I purge the parts that no longer serve me. Remaining fluid in my approach keeps me in tune. I am listening to myself.

Support doesn't always come from those around you. And although it is easier to second guess that bra-over-top look, that's why self-image is so important; it stands alone as we do the same. It gives room for us to walk into the night with confidence and speak for ourselves.

I wanted to unlearn the standards of gender as expression by picking and choosing my standard. I want to have an aesthetic that says, "Fuck your concern. I know what I'm doing." I want my styling strategy to be a secret between me and me, and others are free to enjoy my own personal red underwear if they choose.

TO BRIDGET JONES, JUST AS SHE IS

Toju Adelaja

Romantic comedies made me the woman I am today, for better, and for worse. Sure, my parents raised me, but so did Nora Ephron and Richard Curtis. Often, when we discuss the impact of romantic comedies we do so in a negative way- that they give women unrealistic expectations that skew our expectations and understandings of love and romance. And maybe that's true. But I also think they can teach us to want and expect more from love, and one of my favourite romcoms, *Bridget Jones's Diary* is up there as one of the best when it comes to this.

Bridget Jones's Diary is one of my comfort movies for many reasons. I'll start with the obvious- it's delightful. It's hilarious and brilliantly written, and features stellar performances from a truly iconic cast, from Jim Broadbent playing Bridget's father, to Colin Firth and Hugh Grant, both veritable romcom legends (and the likely source of the myth that British men are the epitome of charm) playing her love interests. It's also incredibly 'British' in its humour, which, despite being quite acerbic in nature, warms this British girl right up like a cup of hot chocolate. However, I think the reason why Bridget Jones usually gets turned on particularly when I'm feeling quite low is because… she makes me feel pretty great about myself.

Sure, things may not be looking up for me, but at least I'm not quite as much of a mess as Bridget. Bridget makes all the mistakes and embarrasses herself in all these various ways so that I don't have to. And what's even better, is that despite it all, despite her being a certifiable disaster from start to finish, Bridget gets her happy ending. This film makes the brave decision to present to you a flawed, chaotic female character and have her be deserving of love, by both her love interest and her friends and family... just as she is.

In the pilot episode of one of my very favourite shows, *Mad Men*, Ken Cosgrove, one of the account executives, is lightly questioned by his co-workers after making a series of in-the-60s-could-be-considered-playfully-misogynistic comments in the elevator all while Peggy, the new girl overhears. Cosgrove, played by Aaron Staton defends himself to his co-workers when they fear she could be assigned to one of them as a secretary "You got to let them know what kind of guy you are. Then they'll know what kind of girl to be." It's alarming, given that the show is set in the 1960s, how much I had latched onto that idea, especially when navigating relationships in my teens. I was a chameleon of sorts, adapting myself, my speech, my style, my interests, and my behavior to whatever guy I was interested in at the time. However, Bridget Jones, once more being the perfect fictional older sister, shows me that I can fearlessly be myself. The right guy will follow, and not the other way round.

I discovered *Bridget Jones's Diary* one evening, having just arrived from a long journey back home after a summer programme at Oxford. On the train back, I'd just had my romcom, 'Before Sunrise' dreams rudely and brutally dashed. I'd struck a connection with a cute boy I'd met at the summer programme, and we'd managed to develop the seedlings of a 'more than friendship' in the few times we'd met. Fortuitously, we found ourselves on the same train home; as despite it somehow never coming up in conversation, it turned out we were actually from the same town but had simply never met. It felt like the stars, Richard Linklater and Nora Ephron from beyond the grave herself, were all aligned. Why else did this cute, ambitious boy, who was nerdy, but confident and charming and my age, and from the same non-descript town in Kent as me somehow end up on the same prestigious summer programme as me, if it wasn't meant to be? The best part was, we had the almost 2-hour train journey home to actually get to know each other. To see if this connection could last longer than a series of 10-minute conversations and brief quips yelled over the blare of 'Wild Thoughts' across the dancefloor.

As a rom-com fanatic even at seventeen, I was convinced that this was the beginning of mine. However, over the hour, it became clear as day that we were actually extremely incompatible. By the end of the journey, we couldn't even pretend that we had any desire ever to see each other again, and we parted ways at the station with a curt and stilted goodbye. The nail in the proverbial coffin came during what I didn't realise was quite a heated debate. Over what, I can't quite remember, likely for my own sanity. During which he said, no, spat, with a curled lip and a derisive tone that I will never forget: 'Wow you're really opinionated aren't you?' He said it like I'd committed a crime, and even though we were both sitting down, eye to eye, I felt about two feet tall. I was instantly deflated, the thrill of the back and forth, which I had been enjoying, replaced with mild embarrassment.

I had gotten a bit too passionate. Too loud, too much. At the time, I felt like I would always be seen that way, and I was destined to forever scare off every guy I liked because of my clear inability to behave like a normal person.

I sat in my living room, with my sweating tub of Ben and Jerry's chocolate fudge brownie ice cream, still feeling like 'a lot,' I figured I might as well watch this iconic movie and finally see what all the fuss was about. I had no idea I'd just picked the perfect movie to snap me out of the mood I was in. Not just because I was a little bit miserable and needed the pick me up, but because I needed to understand that for the right person, I wouldn't ever feel too passionate, too opinionated, or too much. Like Mark and Bridget, he too would like me, very much, 'just as I am.'

Bridget Jones's Diary initially presents itself as a typical relatable heroine story- she starts the film determined to 'improve' herself, as we all tend to at the beginning of a new year. She sets goals to lose weight (watching in 2022, the presentation of the objectively slim Renée Zellweger as 'overweight' in any way now seems uncomfortably anachronistic), smoke less, and make better choices in men. It is typical of most stories to be structured this way: protagonists must learn some lesson or become better people in some way over the course of their journey towards their happy ending with their love interest. They must change, in some way, whether that change is major or minor. A 'makeover scene,' where the main character's outward appearance is changed is often featured, and usually, through that, they become more visible and desirable to their love interest.

In *27 Dresses*, Katherine Heigl's character learns to stop being such a doormat, and that eases her into her relationship with James Marsden's. In *My Big Fat Greek Wedding*, Nia Vardalos' 'Toula' goes through a complete physical and professional transformation, and that gets her noticed by her love interest, and gives her the confidence to pursue a relationship with him. However, while I love a 'makeover scene' as much as the next person, I have always seen them as slightly problematic. Not because there's necessarily anything wrong with wanting to better yourself, but because I just don't appreciate the suggestion that women ever need to fundamentally change themselves in order to be worthy of love.

I think the very best love stories, the very best romcoms, are those where the female protagonist actually doesn't grow. Where their gaining of love and their love interests' affections has absolutely nothing to do with any professional or personal growth or change. It sounds backwards, and possibly a bit antithetical to a more 'typical' story structure altogether, but there's something incredibly romantic about watching a character being loved, just as they are.

In *10 Things I Hate About You*, Kat remains 'difficult' from the beginning to the end of the film. Sally's numerous neuroses actually feature in Harry's declaration of love at the end of *When Harry Met Sally*. And in *Pride and Prejudice*, the book on which *Bridget Jones's Diary* is loosely based, it becomes clear that Elizabeth's personality is not necessarily the problem or anything that must be changed, but rather her understanding of Mr. Darcy.

Bridget does achieve professional success within the story - but that's *despite* her relationships with men, and has almost nothing to do with the central love story. You can see that Darcy already likes Bridget fairly quickly into the film- that is, even before he gets to experience her 'transformation' of sorts. She's still resolved to lose weight and is still incapable of behaving 'properly' in public, but he clearly doesn't care. The fact that Bridget's 'makeover scene' of sorts is entirely played for laughs indicates that Bridget 'changing' simply does not in any way matter to the story.

I recently rewatched the scene from *Bridget Jones* where Mark first awkwardly tells Bridget that he 'likes her very much just as she is' on YouTube, and was surprised to see that a certain comment got as many likes as it did. The comment said that they never understood, nor was it ever really explained, why Mark liked Bridget so much. And I think that just indicates a gross misunderstanding of the film. It's never explained why specifically Mark likes Bridget, just as she is, but I don't think it requires an explanation. He likes her... just as she is. She doesn't need to change, she doesn't need to become more confident, or dress differently. There's no pivotal moment where he starts to see her differently. He just sees more of her, being exactly herself, and finds himself increasingly endeared to her and enamoured with her, just as the audience does.

The key moment in which you realize that Darcy really *does* love Bridget is when he finds her at home, covered in what can only be described as 'green mush' - clear evidence that whatever it is she's doing, she's probably doing it badly, you can almost see the cartoon heart eyes take over his face when he sees her attempt at the 'dinner' she's trying, and failing, to put together. He takes over, trying to salvage it as best he can. It needs to be said that Mark likes Bridget because she's a mess and he finds it endearing. You never get any indication that he's laughing at her, or finds her ridiculous in any way- he just wants to help her. When her friends arrive and attempt to eat the 'dinner,' they make a toast, also appreciating and loving Bridget 'just as she is.' It's pretty beautiful how, throughout, there's never any indication from Bridget's friends or Mark that she needs to be anything different than exactly who she is.

This is the difference between them and Bridget's other love interest, Daniel Cleaver (played delectably by Hugh Grant), with whom she always seemed to be trying to change herself for. Efforts which, in the end, were clearly never quite enough. Additionally, Bridget always seemed to be something of a curiosity to Daniel, something to 'try out' and have a bit of a laugh with, rather than an actual woman to be taken seriously, which Mark does right from the start. You can best see this during a scene where they're both attending a dinner party at a friend's house. While the other guests are rather insensitive to Bridget's clear discomfort as the only single person at a dinner table full of couples, Mark is the only one who actually notices and sticks up for her.

Far from Mark not having a 'reason' or 'justification' to fall in love with Bridget, the film makes it clear that no such reason or justification is required. What we get to know of the character- in all her chaos, social awkwardness and humour, is exactly why he falls in love with her and is more than enough reason. Even if it is all a bit quick, as viewers, also having only experienced Bridget over the course of the hour and thirty-seven minute run time- she really is quite easy to fall in love with.

A while ago I remember tweeting that I was growing tired of Hollywood's seeming infatuation with high school set romances, focusing on teenagers. 'They're dumb! I don't care!' I said. While that may seem rich coming from me, as, at twenty-two, I'm certainly not so far removed from the tedium and emotional immaturity of teenage romances, I do maintain that it's much more interesting to watch actual adults, with baggage, and a better grip on who they are, interact in romantic relationships. Even though so much of the plot hinges on Bridget being perceived as ridiculous, there is still an air of maturity surrounding her relationships, particularly with Mark. I like to imagine that by the time you're in your 30s, you're a lot more comfortable in your own skin (or at least I hope I will be), and Bridget is nothing if not that, especially by the end of the film. These days, I'm a lot less fearful of someone not liking me for me, probably because I've become a lot more set in my ways in my old age. Looking back on it with new eyes, pretending to be someone you're not just to be appealing to somebody else is simply unsustainable. It's draining, and it robs you of a lot of joy, and *potential* joy that you *could* have if you simply committed to waiting to find someone who likes you for you. I'll be honest, it's a challenge sometimes, but now, more than ever, I'm certain that this wait for my 'Darcy' will be more than worth it when I eventually find him.

Bridget meets Darcy in an objectively ugly outfit, we realize he really does quite like her after she's made a huge mistake at work, and their love story ends with her once again embarrassing herself by her chasing after him through the snowy streets of London in just her knickers. Bridget does not become more sophisticated, or palatable, or really, any different in any significant way over the course of their love story, and that's exactly the point. *Bridget Jones's Diary* is, to me, one of the more excellent romcoms because it does not require anything of its protagonist for her to be deserving of love. For once women are able to see a story where they are deserving of a fairytale ending without the need for the big 'makeover scene'. You might want to change, for yourself, and there's nothing wrong with that, but sometimes, have the courage to be you, flaws and all.

Elizabeth Teets

CHILD SLUPPERS IN HALLOWEENLAND: THE TERROR OF *HOCUS POCUS*

Ella Gale

My favorite thing on earth is an impeccable theme. Put me in a restaurant designed to look like a 19th century gold mine and I am happy. If I could, I would live in a Rainforest Café. When I visit an expensive home, I think to myself "this is great, but how good can it be if they're not sleeping in a bed tucked inside a towering fake Kapok tree?" My inability to keep house plants alive has never stifled these dreams, although for now I have to settle for tiki bars and Disneyland.

One of my favorite childhood movies excels at theming. *Hocus Pocus* is wall-to-wall Halloween, of the witchy New England flavor. It's essentially a haunted hayride for delivering the campy villainy of Bette Midler, Kathy Najimy, and Sarah Jessica Parker as witches, known as the Sanderson sisters. The core plot revolves around Max (Omri Katz), the new kid in town, accidentally bringing the evil Sanderson sisters back from the dead. A bad way to start things off at a new school. Max has to find a way to kill the witches while impressing his crush and keeping his little sister safe.

The pleasures of the comedic performances abound, from Midler's conniving coven frontwoman, to Najimy's child-slurping but also people-pleasing fixer, to Parker's idiot songstress. They're fine on their own, but together they're a vicious treat, like a candy bar with a razor inside.

If I could vacation inside any movie, I might choose this one, with its windswept autumnal graveyards, impeccably decorated mansions, and bumping house parties. The movie is set in Salem, Massachusetts, and right from the start it's unapologetic about its thesis: the Puritans were right, and those witches were real. Although this rigid moral posturing is quickly bent under the weight of jokes about how the witches can only be brought back from the dead by a *virgin*.

My sister and I wore out a VHS tape of the movie, which we taped when it played on ABC in the mid-90s. The lead performances - scenery-chewing, down to the bone - are an easy distraction from the movie's scares. As an adult, it's hard to pick out the terror from behind the campy Halloween bunting. But the movie does, after all, begin with three witches tying a child down, force-feeding her a nauseous potion, and drinking her soul until she dies. In short order, the movie features a public execution, a pet cat flattened paper-thin across the sidewalk, immolation inside a pottery kiln, kids awaiting torture in swinging cages (shout out to the Iceman) and a zombie with his mouth sewn shut, an image that still needles its way under my skin. None of it is graphic, but when you're a kid, being buried in the dirt for two hundred years with your mouth sewn shut is more real when it happens in your head.

No fear is deeper than childhood fear. Before you've been overexposed to life, it's easy to believe. Encouraging belief in children has always struck me as unhinged. If a cheerful white-haired man can climb down your chimney and leave you a present, what shaggy many-legged creature might slip in through the ash behind him? When you're a kid, there's a bigness to the world, a sense of things stretching out in all directions, including the dark places. There's a vastness to life and a mystery to the world around you - and I'm not talking about chipper childhood wonder. I'm talking about an extraterrestrial, Lovecraftian endlessness.

The other movie that terrified me as a child—another constantly re-winded VHS - was the Night on Bald Mountain segment of *Fantasia*. More of a tone poem than a story, the segment features a black bat-winged demon the size of a mountain rising from slumber and raising the souls of the dead from a nearby village. These naked, skeletal figures race to the mountain, where they dance for the capricious demon's pleasure amid hellfire before church bells scare them back to their pits. A fun little children's flick.

Animated drawings of skeletal horses and bare-chested harpies no longer scare me, but the images of flowing ghosts and transformed imps cast into the fires of hell remain striking. I must have seen the segment once, but after that I can only remember being too scared to watch it, fast-forwarding through the segment as soon as the hippos had finished their pas de deux in Dance of the Hours, relieved and bored by the Ave Maria priests at the end.

My childhood was haunted by its own writhing demons. I had leukemia when I was very young. Although I was sick enough to go be hospitalized, that part of my life is almost entirely hidden from me. I have only two memories of the experience: One, I got a troll doll with pink hair and a pink gemstone bellybutton when I was in the hospital. And two, I once had a large bandage on my back, which interfered with bath time. Otherwise my illness made no impositions on my long-term memory. It's an ominous blank spot on the map of my life. *Here there be dragons.* I barely know how sick I was - although I know that my parents turned down a Make-a-Wish trip to Disneyland for me because they were pretty sure I was going to live.

This early medical distress might be why the little girl's death at the start of this movie frightened me so much, because she is forced to drink something foul and sickening. No one ever drank my soul when I was young (as far as I know), but I did have chemicals pumped into my body. I still have a scar on my chest from a broviac catheter, which as an adult I have largely used as a watermark for deciding when a shirt is too slutty.

Another scene from a horror movie that scares me deeply - that still holds up, in fact - is the mouse transformation from *The Witches.* It came out when I was three, but I hopefully didn't watch it until I was a mature eight or nine. Early in the movie, a young boy named Luke is grabbed by witches, held down, and force fed a potion that turns him into a mouse. The transformation is not particularly scary, but the force feeding is an absolute horror, as silk-gloved hands paw and pry Luke's mouth open, sticking the bottle almost halfway down his throat. The adults in the room - ostensibly there for a children's welfare conference - smack him around and laugh at his pain.

When I was young, I pictured death not as sleep, but as trying to sleep, as having to lie very still in absolute darkness forever. The evangelical neighbor girls' earnest attempts to convert me imploded spectacularly after they told me there was no food in heaven. I remain impressed by those little girls' honesty. No false promises of endless taco parties from them, not even for their friend's immortal soul.

The horror in *Hocus Pocus* folds up by the end into a neat orange-and-black bow. The witches die, the flattened cat reinflates, and the zombie is actually a nice guy. *Yes, there be dragons here, but they're actually very friendly and they're starting a new barbecue business.*

The little girl who dies at the beginning of *Hocus Pocus* returns as a ghost to pull her brother's spirit into a final death. The movie telegraphs a sense of peace and light, but those ghosts don't know anything about that last horizon, and neither do we. It's the final blank spot on the map. For all the laughs and festive autumnal cheer, *Hocus Pocus* will remain a movie that scared me.

I WANTED TO *BRING IT ON*

Michelle Theil

I don't remember the first time I watched *Bring It On*. The film was first released in 2000, when I was barely two years old, and I can't imagine that my parents would have thought it was an appropriate film for a baby to watch in between *Thomas the Tank Engine* and *Bob The Builder*. If I had to guess, I wonder if I came across the DVD while browsing HMV with my dad after a dentist appointment, which was his best way of bribing me to go get my cavities filled, or when I was let loose at the local video rental store with £10, which could get me three for a week.

Despite the murky beginnings of my relationship with *Bring It On*, I watch it at least twice a year or when I'm feeling down, because the sheer joy of watching the competition between the Toros and the Clovers cannot be overshadowed by whatever else is going on in my life. I know the movie intimately, the ins and outs of Kirsten Dunst and Eliza Dushku's borderline homoerotic 'gals pals' friendship, the racial dynamics that I probably didn't appreciate when I was 10 but certainly can criticize now, and the choreography of every routine.

I won't claim that *Bring It On* is the only reason I wanted to be a cheerleader. Growing up watching a million American TV shows and movies filled with cool, popular, gorgeous cheerleaders definitely contributed. *Kim Possible* was a bad-ass superhero and a cheerleader, as was Hayden Panettiere's Claire Bennet in *Heroes*, which I'm sure inspired many a young girl to be a 'girlboss' or a 'bad-ass bitch' before those terms even entered into the mainstream. The short-lived but excellent CW series *Hellcats* featuring Aly Michalka of Aly & AJ fame was also a source of inspiration, not to mention Quinn Fabray (Diana Agron), Santana Lopez (Naya Rivera), and Brittany Pierce's (Heather Morris) singing girl-gang of cheerleaders in *Glee*. More recently, we have been given *Cheer* from Netflix to offer a more in-depth insight into the world of competitive cheerleading, and teen dramas *Dare Me* and *Riverdale* for the more stereotypical yet modern depictions of cheerleading, which only furthered my interest in the sport. All of these shows and films made me want to be a cheerleader, but *Bring It On* and the subsequent movies that spawned out of the franchise were truly the beginning of my obsession with cheerleading.

If in the 22 years since *Bring It On* came out, you haven't yet had the pleasure of seeing this seminal piece of work, here is the gist: Torrance (Dunst) is the new cheerleading captain of the Toros and finds out that the team had previously been stealing routines from a squad called the Clovers at an "inner-city school." The Clovers captain Isis (Gabrielle Union) vows to beat the Toros at the national competition as she's sick of the more affluent white girl squad taking their ideas. On the surface, it is a classic competition between the two squads and we are probably supposed to root for Torrance to rise above those obstacles and beat the Clovers fair and square. But, it goes deeper than that. It is a question of class and race, and the divisions that allow one team to succeed over the other simply because of where they grew up, went to school, and the opportunities they have.

Early on in the film, Torrance and her new teammate Missy (Dushku) visit the Clovers and are confronted by Isis and her team about the theft, believing that Torrance and Missy are doing the same thing. Immediately bringing up the obvious, one cheerleader asks, snarkily, "Were the ethnic festivities to your liking today?"

Torrance is confused, as she (claims she) had no idea the routines were stolen. Isis remarks that the Toros have been stealing their routine for years and then seeing the squad performing them on ESPN when they make it to national competitions, which the Clovers have never been able to do. Speaking about a chant the Clovers invented, Isis says: "I know you didn't think a white girl made that shit up."

It's easy to dismiss *Bring It On* as a quirky comedy about cheerleading with fun dances, stunts, and sassy comebacks but it is an excellent representation of cultural appropriation, years before we even came up with such a term.

White people stealing art and culture from the Black community has happened for ages, and despite this film coming out over two decades ago, what happens in *Bring It On* has not stopped it from happening today. With TikTok for instance, Black content creators have consistently exposed how white TikTok creators have taken their work, such as dance routines, and popularised them without crediting the original inventor. Stars like Addison Rae and Charlie D'Amelio have made millions (Rae made $5 million in 2020) and gained followers from posting viral dance moves, and have later earned movie, TV, and brand deals as a result of those videos. But, the choreography that they used to catapult their careers were taken from Black TikTok stars who are not credited or paid for their work. This persistent theft of their work, without seeing anything lucrative come out of it while white TikTok stars get paid the big bucks, forced Black TikTok creators to go on strike in June 2021 – they refused to make dances for Megan Thee Stallion's 'Thot Shit' and many other popular songs with the hashtag #BlackTikTokStrike to drive the point home. Is *Bring It On* any different?

The majority white cheerleading team Toros stole routines from the majority Black team Clovers and became popular, while the Clovers missed out on the opportunities that came with winning a national sporting competition, such as scholarships to college, exposure from being on national TV, brand deals, better training, etc. Twenty-two years later, *Bring It On* feels more relevant than ever.

TikTok is simply one example, but even current instances of Blackfishing, Asianfishing, and cultural appropriation by white women like Kim Kardashian, Kylie Jenner, Ariana Grande, Little Mix's Jesy Nelson, and hundreds more who take styles, are represented by this film from the beginning of the 21st century. Isis herself comments on this by saying that the Toros steal the Clovers' routines, embody it through their own whiteness, and call it their own, which somehow makes it 'cool.' Braids are considered unprofessional on a Black woman at work, but when Kim Kardashian does it, it's shared countless times on Instagram. Gabrielle Union herself said in 2018 that she was drawn to Isis because of the social justice element of *Bring It On*, while also mentioning that she had wanted to audition for another cheerleading movie called *Sugar and Spice* but because none of the characters were Black, she wasn't allowed to.

As a kid, I obviously wasn't as 'woke' or as well-versed in critical race theory as I am today. I wasn't watching *Bring It On* with the same perspective as I do now. I rooted for Torrance and Missy, because that's what the film told me to do. Over the years though, I realised that while the Toros were not villains or even the anti-heroes of the movie, they are most certainly not victims either. Their positions as the more privileged, white squad, which won year after year because they stole their routines from a less privileged squad that had no chance of defending themselves was mired in the power dynamics of race. The Clovers deserved to win at the end not only because they were excellent cheerleaders with the best routine but also because it was a form of reparation for the injustices they previously experienced. This wasn't something I was able to see when I was younger but, as I grew up, who I rooted for and why changed because of my experiences and the people I interacted with. Ironically, I once wrote a piece defending Sharpay Evans from *High School Musical* as the victim rather than the villain she is portrayed to be but I 100% promise you that I was previously a Gabriella and Troy stan through-and-through.

This changing viewpoint came hand-in-hand with coming to terms with my own identity as a mixed-race person. Growing up and seeing all of these white, blonde cheerleaders positioned as the stars, the winners, all I wanted was to look like them and be like them. But, I wasn't blonde or white. I have dark, almost black hair, and olive skin, and it didn't seem like I would fit in. How am I supposed to be a cheerleader when those cheerleaders fit into a certain archetype that I was never going to be a part of? I dealt with a lot of internalised racism when I was younger, which meant that I didn't like the colour of my skin or my mixed-race identity because I was made to feel like I wasn't pretty enough or good enough to be a part of certain groups – including cheerleading. Beauty standards have historically been very euro-centric, focused on those who were white and blonde, and cheerleading was no different when it was portrayed on screen. If I didn't look like them, I wouldn't be accepted by them. I was similarly rejected by girls in my hometown and at my school for being non-white, and I had no inkling that cheerleading could be any different.

So, for a long time, I pushed my own version of the American Dream to the back of my mind. I'm not American but through a love of literature, reading about the American Dream in books like *The Great Gatsby*, it spoke to me because I didn't desire prosperity or success in the traditional sense but rather the comfort and camaraderie that came with being a cheerleader – which seemed to me only existed in American teen dramas and movies. But, Isis, and the rest of the Clovers were Black, Latina, and other non-white ethnicities – the closest to what I looked liked and identified as – and they won their competition. The third film in the *Bring It On* franchise, called *Bring It On: All or Nothing*, and the fifth film *Bring it On: Fight to the Finish*, also featured a number of non-white, amazing, bad ass cheerleaders too, and I held on to the fact that maybe I could become a cheerleader after all.

My university had a cheerleading squad too, but I was too

scared to try out the first two years I was there. I have anxiety, so it was scary to try something completely new that I had no experience in. I'm not flexible or sporty either, having always been the person reading a book in the corner or writing on my laptop rather than kicking a ball around. When I arrived at the try-outs, I was disappointed to see that many of the people there were also blonde and white and I immediately felt like I didn't belong. My fears about not fitting in grew with every second, and after doing a warm-up and some stunts with a few of the more experienced cheerleaders, I left – without trying out – because I didn't match up to them in skill or appearance. While I am aware that I wasn't going to be perfect at something straight off the bat, I didn't feel comfortable enough to even try but I also felt great shame at letting my fears and anxieties control me. I felt like I had failed, and I never went back to the cheerleading session again. At university, where there are people from so many different backgrounds and ethnicities, it sucked that cheerleading was still the majority white place I had expected it to be while growing up and not seeing much diversity on the screen. There went my cheerleading dreams, *again*.

I often watch *Bring It On* when I'm down, so that night, I watched it along with the rest of the movies in the franchise. In between, I'd listen to the songs written for the *Bring It On* musical written by Lin-Manuel Miranda, Tom Kitt, Amanda Green, and Jeff Whitty, which is excellent. As I sat watching it, I remembered how much I wanted to be a cheerleader and how I wish I could be transported into these films and live their cool high-school lives instead of being the neurotic, wild, writing-obsessed person I really was. The idea of being a cheerleader was so intoxicating to me because it was a gateway to another world – a chance to be athletic, sporty, interesting and, yes, popular too, not to mention being able to shirk uniforms and school clothing policies to wear your cheerleading outfit like a badge of honour. I wanted it all. I was never popular or cool or pretty enough at school and maybe if I had become a cheerleader, I could have been one or all of those things. It took me a while to realise that I was letting my own preconceptions and fears stop me from doing something I wanted to do, and no matter what film and TV told me – and let's be honest, until recently, the industry has always been very whitewashed – anyone could be a cheerleader.

In February 2022, I discovered that there was an adults-only cheerleading squad in London through Instagram. After scrolling through their Instagram account obsessively for a few days, I took a leap and contacted them to come for a session. When I attended, there were so many people who looked like me that I immediately felt at ease and felt like I could be a cheerleader. Although my university was 70% white, London is nearly 50% Black, Asian, and minority ethnic, and I'm sure many of them had similar dreams of being a cheerleader.

I have been cheerleading for nearly four months. I am a base, which means I hold up the girls who get tossed around like a salad (also called flyers) and make sure that I always catch them before they fall. Cheerleading scares me, and it's definitely hard, but it's also fun and so worthwhile to finally stomp around in a cute outfit and do things that sometimes seem impossible. I'm nowhere near the level of either Torrance or Isis, but one day I hope to be part of those cheerleading videos I so love to watch and to watch *Bring It*

On in a whole new light. My experience is nowhere like the movie, because life isn't a movie. There's less chanting or cute dance moves than in *Bring It On*, as the kind of cheerleading is more focused on stunts. But, we do have fun music and there is a strong level of trust and camaraderie when you're trusting each other to catch you and help you hold an entire person up.

Even though it's not exactly like the movie, there's a lot that I need to thank *Bring It On* for. I feel like I've overcome a lot to get to this place, to achieve my own strange version of the American Dream, and I couldn't have done it without the extensive representation and spirit of inclusivity that *Bring It On* brought to cheerleading at a time when it wasn't common or expected. I'm not walking the halls in my cheerleading uniform and becoming popular off the back of it, but that's not so important anymore. *Bring It On* taught me that cheerleading is all about your strength of character and your support for others – both physically and metaphorically.

A JEWISH GIRL'S CATHOLIC IDOL: *SUPERSTAR*

Yaël Krinsky

In my head, Mary Katherine Gallgher and I are best friends. We are not a likely match: she is Irish Catholic, and I come from a Moroccan and Ashkenazi Jewish household. But in my fantasy we become fast friends. After a night of sharing our deepest vulnerabilities, laughing our heads off until one of us spits out a beverage, there comes a moment, and somehow we understand, without having to say it, that our shared aptitude for humor stems from tragedy. We grow older and inevitably become famous for our two-person comedy show called "Two Women, One Deodorant." Money never gets between us.

In real life, Mary Katherine Gallgher is a fictional character in the movie, *Superstar*, created and performed by the inimitable Molly Shannon. Shannon became my television mentor at age 9, to me she was especially soothing when it came to coping with bullying, divorce, puberty, tragedy and feeling like a total and utter failure. I shared her longing for a spectacular, meaningful life; something validating and worthy. I do often wonder if Molly Shannon is aware of just how influential she was to girls like me. Does she know that nine--year-olds were lunging into the iconic "Superstar!" pose? Or that she gave me permission to be wild, comical and…. *weird?*

Superstar, released in 1999 follows a socially awkward, orphaned high school student, Mary Katherine Gallagher (Shannon) who lives with her strict grandmother. She attends a Roman Catholic high school where, in order to get the attention of her popular crush and reach stardom, she enters a talent competition in hopes of winning the grand prize, a chance to be an extra in a movie with positive moral values. Despite her social awkwardness, and unflattering school uniform Mary Katherine Gallagher holds on to one truth: she was born to be a superstar.

The bulk of *Superstar* is spent following Mary Katherine Gallagher as she attends Catholic school, dreaming of stardom and getting her first kiss— practicing on trees and TV screens. The character of Gallagher, originally created by Shannon for *Saturday Night Live*, is most known for her comedic physical presence, going so far as to catapult herself out of her confessional, smelling her own armpits, doing exaggerated prayers, and making her breasts hold hands. I loved how it was something my eyes had never seen before.

For as long as I can remember, my parents were in a constant process of getting divorced. Time can feel rather endless when you're a child. When it came to the holidays, separated-parents Hanukkah was trash. I stopped receiving presents early on while my parents were too busy divorcing. Other kids of divorced parents spoke of the "double presents" holiday, where each parent made an effort to have their own celebration. They'd call me Christmas morning to share all the glorious gifts they'd received. I resented them. It wasn't so much the presents I was missing, but the sense of fitting in somewhere. My upbringing was focused on my Moroccan Jewish side, in a heavily Christian town, and all around me were tales of the magic of Christmas, the power of believing, the happiness that comes from a floor of presents. I tried explaining gelt and dreidels to my friends but truly who the fuck cares about a spinning wooden object and fake money?

To make matters worse, my house sat directly across from an Episcopal church. The priest was the father of a kid I went to school with. In middle school he would have a gossip-rich affair with a kid's mother in the same grade—she was the town's violin teacher. *Ooo la la!* Personally, I didn't see how this changed anything. The Episcopal stone church still stood as a beacon of hope amid all my childhood Christmas dreams.

It was not a particularly pretty church, but it was the only one in the town made of stone. Every Sunday I awoke to the romantic bells and the sounds of children and families coming in and out of service. My absolute favorite time of year to watch outside my window was Christmas. This holiday felt like a barometer for how depressing or happy your life truly was. A way to know you were missing out on *something* even if you didn't know what that something was.

When *Superstar* was released, it became my personal manual. Watching it, I wanted to be more than just as physically funny as Molly Shannon; I wanted to grow into someone admired and inspirational. As I grew into adulthood, I finally realized being funny was not only an emotional outlet, but a mode I fell into when wanting to win people over, feel confident or make people happy.

I gravitated towards Molly Shannon in *Superstar* the way a

72

child gravitates, almost primordially, to certain foods, toys or sounds. Watching her on screen I thought, "This is it, THIS is how I want to be! I found it." Every weekend I would rewatch the movie, and like a magnet, would inch closer and closer to the screen, pausing if needed, studying every bit in my little nine-year-old body, acting out moves, dialogue and jokes. Now at age thirty-two, *Superstar* is the only film I am able to quote from memory.

After months of watching *Superstar*, and moving through the unfortunate motions of my boring, unfamous nine- year-old life, the holidays inevitably approached and they were the hardest. My parents were engrossed in their problems, my siblings were out of the house, it got dark early, and family tradition had been over for years. On Christmas Eve in 2009, I had a date night with my window and the Episcopal church. While my dad was away on a film project, and my mom was doing her usual Christmas nursing shift in the emergency room, I scurried around my house looking for ways to decorate. My house was adorned with deep red-colored Middle Eastern Rugs, buddha fixtures and a piano topped with menorahs, both ancient and new. We had collections of yarmulkes from every bar and bat mitzvah ever attended, and a cabinet full of Shabbat material. Nothing in my house remotely looked like Christmas.

I relied on my mom's largest house plant to pose as a Christmas Tree, which I'd decorated with Christmas lights I purchased. I understood the Christmas Tree to be a signal - like ET's heart light alerting the aliens - I thought Santa would know to come. I thought of it like Noah's ark, "If you build it, they will come." Or more like Field of Dreams, HE will come.

I needed something to stand out in this Jewish Emblem of a household.

Before heading upstairs, I scoured the cabinet and fridge for something to leave Santa and the reindeer. The two best options were pickles and dates. I chose pickles as a juicy and acidic alternative to cookies.

Perched up on my bed, lining the window facing the church, I romantically watched as the church festivities began. Oh how I marveled at this event! I saw kids from school, their parents, neighbors, and grandparents. Every girl was in a dress that had one of those poofy skirt bottoms. I was envious, I was mesmerized. Midnight mass was the dreamiest; it felt like secrecy, magic, and community all at once. The stuff I longed for. As soon as those bells rang, I would move onto the floor, bend my Jewish knees to the ground, hold my hands in prayer position on my bed à la Mary Katherine Gallagher, and pray to God. This is not the typical prayer position for my people.

"Dear God" with a very deliberate pause to make sure my voice carried through space and to God's ears before I continued, "please please make Santa come to my house. I beg you. I will do anything, I will be the best child, and I will be the best Jew, just please make him come. I really need it. Thank you. I'm sorry. I love you." I would tuck myself into bed with the utmost confidence He had heard me.

The jerk Santa never came.

My childhood best friend, Taylor Madden, remembers my Mary Katherine Gallagher obsession.

"One time at the Girl Scout building," she messaged me,

"you tried re-enacting the stack of chairs scene where she does the superstar [lunge] and falls over all those folding chairs."

I remember plotting exactly where I'd catapult myself into the metal stack of chairs, considering the absolute best timing for this reenactment. I learned from Molly that timing was critical; it had to be at the right moment, and I had to commit. I flung myself into the chairs, abandoning all physical caution, knowing that my priorities lay in the laugh, not in my safety. The uproar of laughter, even at a young age, felt like the epitome of being alive. So much of my childhood, I felt alone, abandoned and lost. But at that moment, I was capable of *something*.

I went on to do these little "skits" at school, parties, and on playdates, seizing any chance to perform. Any chance to feel worthy and validated. One week, Ms. Gretta, my middle school English teacher, let my friends and me eat lunch in her classroom - unsupervised. It was the only subject I could remotely excel in, I like to think I was one of her favorites. I was the only student who interpreted *Sound of Silence* by Simon and Garfunkel to her liking. A definite warning sign. I never got around to eating my lunch that day, having spent the entire time traipsing around with my pants pulled up so high you could see my butt and vaginal outlines. I would bash into walls as if by accident, lunge into Superstar poses, invent characters—mixing in my own made up moves. I was some amalgam of Mary Katherine Gallagher, Molly Shannon and Yaël Benizri Krinsky.

In Molly Shannon's memoir, *Hello Molly*, she reveals a major tragedy of her childhood, which ultimately played a large role in her career and inspired the character of Mary

75

Katherine Gallagher. She explains her connection between abandoning physical caution in performance with pain and grief. The moments she flung herself into bathroom stalls or metal chairs, were moments that felt good, not just because it made people laugh, but because being transgressive and chaotic felt good. To be reckless, for Molly Shannon, and for me, was to express things left unsaid or unresolved; to repurpose it into commitment and laughter.

At age thirteen, I was sexually assaulted, words I have not written so permanently before. At age seventeen I became ill, and suffered thirteen years until an eventual endometriosis diagnosis and surgery. Comedy, and the delight of almost maniacal laughter, was a way I could prove I was still whole. It tethered me to the only part of me leftover.

In my case, Molly Shannon literally "paved the way." When people express moments of sheer certainty, that is how I felt upon watching *Superstar*. I knew that physical comedy was a language I was so happy to learn not only existed, but was ok for me to inhabit.

All these years, I noticed a similar thread in myself— the physical recklessness, desire to please, search for validation through humor - not knowing that the person I had most idolized was teaching me, not only a means of resiliency, but of success.

I'm often asked why I love *Superstar* so much. Is it just that physical comedy by nature is funny? Was I just young and silly? Upon reading *Hello Molly* and learning more about what influenced Molly Shannon, I knew those parts of her are what most drew me - the primordial pull. I didn't have to know why as a child; the dreaminess of being magnetized to something without reason. I noticed in her what I noticed in myself: the palpable chaos and uncontrollable parts of life, which inevitably push at the seams of our physical body, coming out as unmanaged as they once existed within us.

Though I don't advise making out with a tree in public, or bursting out made-for-TV movie monologues, I do encourage being as unabashedly yourself and potentially paving your own way, as Molly Shannon once taught me. I am still not a full *Superstar*, but I am on my way.

THE FIRST WIVES CLUB AND THE DYNAMICS OF GIRL GROUPS

Lana Schwartz

One of my favorite jokes to make is:

"If you and your group of high school female friends didn't have a name for your clique, you weren't that close."

As a young woman, particularly before you're old enough to drink or do drugs or have sex, there are few highs quite like finding yourself enmeshed in a new group of female friends. All we want as teenage or tweenage girls is to be accepted – to have sleepovers to attend or girls with whom we can wear matching outfits. Plus, there's strength in numbers. Becoming part of a group, whether or not it's the popular one (although it certainly helps if it's the popular one), provides a buffer against potential bullies and other types of an alienation. It's human instinct: We want to be accepted by the herd, and if the herd calls itself *Juicy Girls* because every member wears Juicy Couture, and therefore everyone knows and recognizes a Juicy Girl, well, all the better. How many times have you heard a girl or woman coo to another "I'm obsessed with you" or "We're *exactly* the same." Being female can be a lonely experience; the knowledge that someone sees us, truly sees us, can be intoxicating.

At that age, all you want is the validation that you're normal. Whatever sort of intrusive thoughts you've had about the second-oldest brother from *Malcolm in the Middle* have to be normal if someone else is having them too.

Throughout my life, I have been part of a few different girl groups, of varying levels of popularity within our social strata. My senior year of high school, I was a member of one such group. We referred to ourselves as the Bare Vs (you can guess why, but please know I shudder as I type this). We had numbers based on when we joined the group. I was number 13, but from what I recall, our count at one point went as high as 18, so while I might not have been far from first, I also was decidedly not last. We even had matching sweatpants decrying our affiliation (I believe my pair is still at the bottom of a closet somewhere).

We were so thrilled to be part of something that we were willing to forsake our names for numbers.[1] I wasn't present for the Bare Vs initial formation, but from what I understand, the whole thing was borne out of some sort of late night shaving party at someone's house.[1] Filled with that pent up, reckless energy teenage girls have, always in need of an outlet, we seek our thrills wherever we can find them; for this group of Jewish teenage girls, it was by way of the blade. While the other girls in the group had to show their work, so to speak, I was officially made a member so late, that by that point, they took whatever I told them about the hair on my vagina in good faith.

[1] I don't personally know if cisgender heterosexual boys or men beyond the fictional men of Entourage and the real men of the Pussy Posse/Wolfpack organize themselves taxonomically, but I think this is why a lot of them start bands.

A lot of us look back on what we did in our adolescence and say "Well, that was stupid." I knew the bare V's was stupid *even back then.* I went to a New York City public high school with a student population that counted as high as 4,500. There were so many of us, we were on a split schedule, the hours of our school day shifting each year; I never once had a lunch period; and the hallways were so crowded, students regularly got pickpocketed. There were far too many of us for there to be any kind of *real* social strata. There was no football team, and ergo, no pep rallies, and no homecoming. This was – and is – a good thing. Despite the lack of traditional high school social hierarchy, I was lucky enough to have a strong group of friends – and yes, we did give our social circle a name, but it was an acronym of our initials, so it was *dignified.* (For the purposes of this story, I'll call us MASH.) Yet there was still part of me that longed for the normalcy of a standard, suburban high school experience, the kind I'd grown up seeing in my favorite TV shows like *Dawson's Creek* and *One Tree Hill.*

The Bare V girls were not my high school classmates, but rather girls that I met through my participation in a Jewish youth group, beginning in 9th grade. Compared to my high school, the youth group had a social strata so strong and so dense, it was practically a class system. And while I'd always been friends with the Bare V girls, there was an invisible line between us: They were popular and I was not. (Or perhaps I should put it this way: They were "hot" and I was not.) So perhaps you can see why I'd be willing to cement myself as a member of some sort of concrete grouping. It was unspoken, but the higher the girl's number, the closer she was to the flames of the inner circle. At 13, I was just lucky to catch some embers. In some ways, this felt normal to me. So many movies and TV shows I loved mirror this sort of relationship, wherein the peripheral characters live in service to the protagonists, lucky if they can pick up a C-story that week. I believe the sort of energy my friends had is what we today refer to as "Main Character Syndrome."

Growing up, I did have at least one positive example of female friendship wherein the women didn't mirror each other, or simply exist as a sounding board for the lead: *The First Wives Club*.

I can't remember the first time I saw *The First Wives Club*, but I can't remember a time in my life before I loved the movie. Like so many of my favorite 90s movies[2] – *A League of Their Own, While You Were Sleeping, Troop Beverly Hills, Beaches*, and the Nora Ephron Big Three – it felt like it was constantly playing on loop on one of the three televisions in our two-bedroom apartment throughout my childhood.

The above films notwithstanding, female characters were frequently indistinguishable. For me, the go-to example of this is The Ashleys from the cartoon *Recess*, who were the girl equivalents of lemmings. And of course, there's the modern classic *Mean Girls*, wherein Regina George's henchwomen had barely discernible qualities beyond "stupid" and "insecure" (this is not to disparage *Recess* or *Mean Girls*, two texts for which I have great reverence). All too often I'd see actresses saddled with the "best friend role," wherein she doesn't have much to do except crack jokes and act as a sounding board

[2]The movies for the girls, gays, and theys.

for the lead. It was also, for some reason, very important that she have brown hair. While this was disappointing, I did find it relatable. Dodging various love interests was not a personal pastime, but using humor as a defense mechanism? Yes, yes, a million times yes.

The First Wives Club finds Annie (Diane Keaton), Brenda (Bette Middler), and Elise (Goldie Hawn) reuniting after decades of estrangement following the loss of their best friend, Cynthia. Each of the women married not self-made men, but men who were shaped and molded by *them*. And once their husbands sapped up everything they could from these women, they ditched them for younger models. It's absurd, it's obscene, and it's a tale as old as time.

In search of revenge, the three women form the titular First Wives Club. Together they pull the rug out from under each of their respective ex-husbands. I have long said that as a child I never really pictured myself married, yet I always aspired to be a well-kept divorcée, with a wit as dry as the gin in my martini. The idea that you need to be married to someday be divorced didn't really cross my mind. I believe I have *The First Wives Club* and Nora Ephron's general existence to thank for these aspirations – as of yet to be realized, but still today firmly held.

I loved all of the film's set pieces, I loved the way it portrayed the New York City I grew up in (unrecognizable today), and as a young Jewish girl, I even loved that Deborah's son has a bar mitzvah (representation!). Of course, because I am a human being with a pulse, I especially loved the movie's closing number set to Lesley Gore's "You Don't Own Me," and the way the women sing without abandon, having finally, at long last, become fully realized versions of themselves.

When I re-watch the movie, one thing that strikes me is how, early in the film, Brenda accurately assesses their situation. "We are a group," she says, and just like any girl group actually worth its salt, each of the women have a different role they play. These three women don't try to emulate each other, because each of them has their own distinct personality, and they're better off for it. And while we don't get to spend too much time with the ill-fated Cynthia, we do know that she was, out of all of them, "the most likely to succeed," leading the audience to believe that when the triangle was still a square, she had her own distinct corner.

Because these women are so different – Elise a vain actress, Brenda a bawdy housewife, Annie meek and shy – they bump up against each other. They don't always get along, and certainly none of them are telling each other how *perfect* they are, but it's because of this that they drive each other to be better. If Elise only hung out with Hollywood types, or Annie with pushover Connecticut wives, they would stay that way forever. No one would confront Elise about her out of control drinking, or push Annie to pursue what she wants, or encourage Brenda to be softer, more forgiving. When the women first realize they want to take revenge against their husbands ("We helped them rise, we can help them fall"), they're unsure at first: So many people have told them that their best days are behind them that they've started to believe it. Elise implores them to think about everything they could achieve if all of the first wives in the world joined forces. Brenda says they'd still need "one amazing attorney," but Elise stands firm. "All we need is us," she says. Together, they each bring something different to the table. Together, they are greater than the sum of their parts.

As we grow older, sometimes we ask ourselves why we're still friends with the people with whom we surround ourselves. If we met them now, would we still become close? Are we holding on to a vestige of the past, or something else? When it comes to *The First Wives Club*, it might seem as though it's the latter, given that the women have drifted apart over the last 30 years, but eventually they come to see that they need each other. In fact, odds are good their reunion might not have ever happened at all, had their friend Cynthia not a) made it her last wish for them to take care of each other, and b) served as a cautionary tale for the toll loneliness can take on a person.

The movie's central conflict hinges not around the men in their lives, but the fact that an insult from a friend you love, respect, and admire hurts more than if it came from anyone else. They have the power to lift each other up, but also, by that same token, to tear each other down.

Suffice to say, I have lost touch with the rest of the Bare Vs. I fell out with them during and after college, and in the great migration from Facebook to Instagram and other various social platforms, I lost my ability (and interest) in giving anyone's social media profile a cursory glance. I believe some intergroup friendships remain, as they always do with cliques, both big and small. I most certainly can't speak to anyone's grooming habits.

However, I am lucky enough to still remain a member of MASH today, although we've long since stopped calling ourselves by any sort of umbrella name. I'd say when we were younger, maybe our qualities did mesh together more, our personalities still malleable. But as we've grown older, we've begun to fully shade in the outlines of who we are, rendering each of us more distinct than the year before. Where our high school interests heavily overlapped (watching *Get Over It* and going to Applebee's after school), today they vary widely, from staying in and playing board games to attending DIY concerts in bar basements.

I'd argue that just as in *The First Wives Club*, it's these differences that make for a stronger friendship; ones that aren't without their complications, or their challenges, but are all the more rewarding. My friends have shown me endless kindness through gestures big and small, like the time my friend flew halfway across the country at a moment's notice to attend my mother's funeral, or when another tracked down Judy Blume and got her to sign a copy of *Summer Sisters* as a gift to me for my 30th birthday – the first without my mom. They've taught me how to be more patient and kinder to myself and others. Hopefully, I've taught them something about which actors are Scientologists.

Friendship can take many different forms. To everything there is a season, and a time and purpose under heaven, etc. We all get different things from different people in our lives. But for me, the friendships that are the most significant are the ones that are put to the test and still pass every time. We might need to go our separate ways sometimes, but we can always come back together and laugh like we have for years, over a meal or while we watch an old favorite like *She's the Man*.

And ultimately, should the time come, there's no one I'd rather dance with down a cobblestone street, singing "You

Don't Own Me (remix by Cardi B and Megan Thee Stallion)."

NORA, MEG AND ME: DISCOVERING THE POWER OF FEMALE FRIENDSHIP IN THE EPHRON-RYAN ROM-COMS

Meg Walters

There are two main characters in every rom-com. There's the woman on top of the Empire State Building waiting for the mysterious, sensitive widow she heard on the radio. Then there's the quirky 'ShopGirl' caught in a digital romance with the mysterious NY152. And, of course, there's Harry and Sally.

These are the love stories from the (unofficial) Nora Ephron-Meg Ryan rom-com trilogy — *Sleepless in Seattle, You've Got Mail* and *When Harry Met Sally*.

Ephron is widely credited with resurrecting the romantic comedy and setting the bar for rom-coms to come, while Ryan, her frequent rom-com heroine, has gone down in history as the undisputed queen of the genre.

As a Millennial who came of age in a Y2K era of increasing digitization and uncertainty, it was this movie trilogy that reeled me into a lifelong love of rom-coms. I yearned for the nostalgic, quaint simplicity of Ephron's version of New York in the '90s. I strove to emulate Ryan's plucky optimism that always seemed to come out in a snooty I-told-you-so type of air. I started talking wistfully about children's bookshops and Cary Grant movies and wagon wheel coffee tables and Zabar's and paprikash and garnishes. And, naturally, I fell head over heels with the love stories.

I return to these movies far more often than anyone probably should. For me, there's nothing like accompanying Meg on a stroll through the Upper West Side in the fall to distract from the 'real world.' But as I approach my 30s, my focus has drifted away from the romantic relationships and towards the platonic ones. Hidden within each of Ephron's rom-coms is a delightful, vibrant female friendship that trickles along below the surface of the romantic love stories. Yes, Ephron may be famous for her portrayal of romance, but each rom-com is also an ode to the steadfast, vitalizing power of female friendship.

In the world of the rom-com, the best friend is usually there to provide a foil for the main character. One moment they may offer the comic relief, the next, they may be cast in the role of the straight man. They are, for the most part, two-dimensional caricatures, destined to exist only to play off the leading lady and, ultimately, to guide her through her journey towards happily ever after.

On the surface, Ephron follows the blueprint to a tee.

And yet, while this trio of Ephron besties do play a practical, structural role, appearing sporadically throughout their respective films offering quippy one-liners and gently shoving Meg in the direction of either Tom or Billy, they are also dazzling, iconic characters in their own right.

You have Carrie Fisher's exuberant, slightly messy Marie in *When Harry Met Sally*. Perpetually dating a married man and whipping out her rolodex of available guys, the excitable, scatty Marie is the perfect sidekick to the uptight and prim Sally. Who else could have summed up the horror of being a Single Woman with such blunt panache: "All I'm saying is that somewhere out there is the man you are supposed to marry. And if you don't get him first, somebody else will, and you'll have to spend the rest of your life knowing that somebody else is married to your husband."

Inspired by Bette Midler, Rosie O'Donnell's fast-talking, screwball-esque Becky in *Sleepless in Seattle* has all but given up on love thanks to her dull and disappointing second husband. Unlike Ryan's ultra romantic Annie, Becky, with a characteristic blunt shrug, can say things like, "Your destiny can be your doom — just look at me and Rick."

Then there's Heather Burns's sullen, sardonic Christina in *You've Got Mail.* Christina, the sloth-like assistant of the Shop Around the Corner, gives us Wednesday Addams with a twist of arch humor. She's the ideal contrast to Ryan's perpetually sunny Kathleen.

But while these three idiosyncratic best friend characters are undoubtedly iconic (thanks in part to the scripts of the Ephron sisters and also to the inspired performances that bring them to life), it is, ultimately, the bond they share with their incarnation of Meg Ryan that has, for me, begun to outshine the central romance. It is these female relationships - Marie and Sally, Becky and Annie, Christina and Kathleen - that speak loudest to me now.

Sure, the portrayal of female friendship takes a backseat to the pursuit of falling in love with a man - the three films just barely squeak through the infamous Bechdel test. And yet, in Ephron's world, women and their friends have nuanced relationships. The friends of the protagonist are funny, supportive, warm, confrontational, emotional, strong, weird, competitive and loving, sometimes in the space of one scene.

I used to wait with bated breath for those heart-stopping moments of romance. When Harry and Sally would lock eyes across a crowded dance floor at that final New Year's Eve party. When Kathleen would muster up the courage to spit out her insults at Joe at Cafe Lalo. When Annie would muster only a "hello" while following Sam around Seattle.

But these moments have begun to dull in comparison to the moments that capture the slowburn of platonic love. When Sally once again bluntly says, "He's never going to leave her," and Marie once again replies, "You're right, you're right, I know you're right." When Kathleen and Christina conspire about cybersex or the rooftop killer while opening up the shop. When Becky and Annie simultaneously mouth along to Cary Grant's lines in *A Night to Remember*, tears streaming down their faces.

In the brunches, the phone calls, the movie nights and the lunch dates, Ephron gives us a glimpse at the most enduring relationships in a woman's life: her friendships.

While her movies are proof that Ephron understood what women want. In my teens and early 20s, I wanted nothing more than that confession of love at a New Year's party or that Empire State Building moment. I wanted the music to swell and my breath to catch. I wanted a great love story. End scene, roll credits.

But the end of a rom-com is just the beginning of a relationship. On the cusp of 30, I've had my fair share of love stories now - some more disappointing than others. And while there's nothing quite like that moment when it all begins, it's become far less interesting to me now than what happens afterwards - and what happens outside of the relationship altogether.

"The thing with friends when you get older is they can't be replaced," Ephron once said.

A best friend knows all the words to your favorite movies. She knows your darkest secrets. She knows how to make you laugh. She will call you out when she needs to. She gives you steadfast companionship like no else really can. And while your relationship with her may not feel as passionate as your romances, as Ephron said, she can't be replaced.

As I've gotten older, my best friends have become more important to me than ever. There's the stylish and smart Amy, who saw me through university with countless plates of sushi, coffee dates, awkward stories and glasses of Sangria and who, from across an ocean, still helps me pick what outfit to wear and what book to read. There's the joyful Eloise, who comes over for a weekly dinner and loves to craft ridiculous schemes that almost always end in agonizing embarrassment. There's the goofy Emma, who gives professional-grade relationship advice and who gracefully understands and accepts every horrible, judgemental thing I say.

Looking back on the moments of great love in my life so far, I'm surprised to find that it's not the stolen glances or first kisses that jump out. Instead, it's the confession shared over a bottle of wine in my first apartment, the roar of laughter from an inside joke and the Taylor Swift singalong.

While her movies are proof that Ephron understood

what women want from romantic love, they are also proof that she understood what women need from their friends. If you look hard enough at Ephron's rom-coms, you'll find another love story bubbling away underneath all of them. Perhaps, she seems to say, the women in our lives are just as important as any romance.

ON *BOOKSMART* REWRITING THE NARRATIVE OF THE TEENAGE GIRL

Anna Sims

Booksmart likes to pretend its big revelation happens on a Los Angeles hiking path overlook. It's a spot where you're surrounded by nature while also looking out at a city, a real have-it-both ways sort of scene. And it's here that perfectionist class president Molly realizes what she and her accomplished activist best friend Amy must do: They need to crash a killer party tonight before graduating from high school tomorrow. They need, Molly says, to "change their stories forever."

Molly and Amy have always focused on grades, followed rules, and carried the mantle of uptight over-achievers. And they did this believing they'd be the ones attending great colleges next fall and living great lives forever after, while their party-loving peers peaked in high school. The problem is that they were wrong. Apparently, their school is some weird Ivy League breeding ground where everyone gets accepted at fancy colleges or offered jobs at Google, regardless of how much they partied.

Cut to Molly freaking out on the best-of-both-worlds overlook. Cut to her determination to party and her seemingly revelatory declaration: "We are not one dimensional. We are smart *and* fun."

When I recently watched *Booksmart* with a friend, she laughed at this scene's suggestion that giving teenage girls two personality traits—smart and fun!—is all it takes to create multidimensional young women. I'll admit, this framing made me laugh, too. Really, could that bar be lower? Then again, movies aren't Virginia Woolf novels. They need plot.

Booksmart's plot isn't special. It's a coming-of-age story where protagonists go on a journey, encounter quirky characters, and overcome setbacks to learn something new. *(What do you know, Molly and Amy *can* be smart and fun! And their partying peers are complex, too!)*

Booksmart's real revelation, the one without a nature-meets-city metaphor or any major declaration: Molly and Amy don't need to party to prove they have dimension. Because from start to finish, they're bookworms, sure. But they're also always confident, kind, funny, bold, multifaceted young women. In this way, *Booksmart* offers a new narrative of how to be a teenage girl.

This message makes *Booksmart* one piece in an emerging narrative-reclaiming puzzle that rewrites the awful lessons society has long taught girls about how to be teenagers and, ultimately, women. Other "pieces" include Jessica DeFino's newsletters, *The Unpublishable* and *The Don't List*, which expose the sexist, racist, and classist scams of beauty culture, along with the podcast *You're Wrong About*, where Sarah Marshall specializes in redefining teens and 20-somethings that history likes to pretend were adult women, from Marie Antoinette to Anna Nicole Smith.

These reclaimed narratives go against everything that I,

a current thirty-two-year-old woman and former teenager of the aughts, was taught. In consuming them, I often find my feelings validated. Because *of course* it was fucked up for us to call Jessica Simpson fat when she wore those high-rise jeans in 2009. I mean, the woman was a size four. *A size four.*

But sometimes, these narratives challenge my understanding of the world, too. In fact, a lot about *Booksmart* challenged my ideas about what teenage girls in film could be. Which is why the movie is so important to me.

Consider when Molly discovers her party-loving peers were also accepted at good colleges: Students in the school's gender-neutral bathroom are playing a game of Fuck-Marry-Kill with a sex doll, beachball, and Molly. They kill Molly, unaware that she's listening from one of the stalls. But then one guy says, "I would make passionate sex to Molly Davidson. I'd just put a bag over her personality." And someone else adds that Molly has "a butter personality."

Watching this scene, I remember the years my friends and I stuffed our normal-sized bodies into those godforsakenly tight low-rise jeans, all to look—and, in doing so, feel—worthy of love and approval. How good would it have felt to be judged by our personalities instead?

And Molly's response? She doesn't cry or stay hidden, like *Mean Girls* and every movie of my youth taught me to do in moments when bullies and bathrooms were involved. Instead, Molly comes out and makes her peers sit in the discomfort they created. "Please, do *not* stop on my account," she says, landing a mic-drop moment that bullied kids of the aughts could only dream about.

Then there's the moment Molly and Amy get dressed

for their life-changing party, and both end up in utilitarian jumpsuits and berets.

"No," Molly says.

"No," Amy echoes.

The first time I watched the movie, I was sure they were upset about the matching outfits. Because when I was in middle school, my parents gave me these cool bowling-style sneakers—which, yes, circa 2002 in Des Moines, Iowa, middle schools, bowling-style shoes were cool. Ask Steve Madden. But my point is that I couldn't wear them because a popular girl in my class already had them. I don't know how I learned this lesson, but seventh-grade me understood it so intimately that those shoes rarely left my closet.

In *Booksmart*, though, after exchanging no's, Molly and Amy say this:

"Who allowed you to be this beautiful?"

"Who allowed *you* to be this beautiful?"

"Who allowed you to take...my breath...away?"

These compliment showers happen throughout the film. And every time, I laugh in amazement but also awe. Because girls didn't talk to each other like that when I was younger, and we *definitely* didn't accept the rare compliments we got. Our go-to response was more like, "Oh my god, no. I look awful."

Never in these narrative-writing moments does *Booksmart* come off as a lesson in "having it all," GirlBossing, or their gender-neutral, but equally problematic cousin, #RiseandGrind, ideas aren't exactly the same, but do feel borne of the same ridiculous premise: That the answer to our problems requires changing or trying harder, not challenging the rules or getting rid of the stereotypes that make it so hard to be a girl in the first place. This is the lesson the plot of *Booksmart* pretends Molly and Amy spend the film unlearning—and *Booksmart* does try hard to present them as girls who believe in stereotypes; that's why the idea that their classmates could party and be smart sets Molly off. It's hard to see that as anything other than a plot device when everything else about Molly and Amy's personalities suggests they're so far beyond that.

The only person unlearning anything when I watch *Booksmart* is me. And that's because I don't see myself in Molly or Amy. I identify with their teacher, Miss Fine. Miss Fine is *Booksmart*'s archetypal cool grownup who has freed herself from society's expectations. And Miss Fine is played by Jessica Williams of *The Daily Show* and *2 Dope Queens* fame, who happens to be exactly my age in real life.

The movie doesn't give Miss Fine much of a backstory, but as soon as I saw her, I knew her entire history. Call it a Millennial bat signal, but behind her well-adjusted eyes, I saw the teenage experience of low-rise jeans and fear of the muffin top. I knew she honed her confident, powerful demeanor the hard way. Because I had to do it that way, too.

In high school, I got straight A's and didn't party. I also really leaned in to a certain kind of 2000's girly girl who liked saying things were *super awesome* and *way cool* and came to school with my makeup done and hair freshly flat-ironed or curled. From being a model student to performing femininity—a concept I wouldn't have a name for until later—I thought I was nailing the teenage girl thing.

But there's no such thing as a perfect teenage girl. It's a

losing battle to try. Or at least, it was for me.

While I thought I was being a good girl, a teacher told me I reminded him of a cartoon character. And my lab partner in chemistry said I should just stand back because I didn't know what I was doing. I guess my having two personality traits—smart and girly—really was too much dimension for the times to process.

When I got to college, I realized just how different the "me" others saw seemed from the person I believed myself to be. And that dissonance between my appearance and actions and who I actually was, well, it wasn't easy to shake off.

Which brings me back to Miss Fine. When Miss Fine drives Molly and Amy to their party, she tells them that she, like me, spent high school trying to be perfect, then spent her 20s rebelling against that persona. (A backstory to which my Millennial bat signal told me, *duh*.)

"I had some really dark moments there in my 20s … Like it was bad," she says. "Did you know I'm banned from Jamba Juice? Like, not a single Jamba Juice. Like, every Jamba Juice."

I didn't get banned from Jamba Juice in my 20s. But I dyed my hair a gross shade of pink. I threw up once on a guy I liked because I was too drunk. I threw up every day on the way to a summer internship because I was too hungover. I got bangs. I made out in dark apartment basements with gross guys, asshole guys, and a few nice guys I wasn't remotely interested in. I did these things because I, like Miss Fine, thought the only way to rectify my past was to make a bunch of ill-conceived decisions in the present.

What I should have done was stop trying or caring about what kind of girl I was before or who I was now. I needed to be like Molly and Amy, to accept myself. To just be myself, whoever that happened to be.

Both Miss Fine and I got there eventually. But that doesn't mean it was easy. It doesn't mean that when Molly and Amy do their compliment exchange thing again outside their party, that Miss Fine doesn't watch them and wonder, *What if their story had been my teenage story, too…*

I think that's why Miss Fine jokes to them, "See you two inside, alright?" Then she laughs and adds, "Imagine if I did, though? Imagine if I just went in?"

"Imagine" is the important word because of what she does next.

What Miss Fine does is actually go to the party. And while she's there, she hooks up with a student. If we take this scene literally, it's bad. Very bad. But everything about the way Miss Fine enters the party tells viewers that something else is going on.

Because High-School-Party-Attending Miss Fine has transformed. She looks awkward and insecure, nothing like the confident woman from the car ride. At this party, she's her teenage self and my teenage self and the teenage self of anyone who wants to be able to look through her insecure eyes and imagine. Imagine the teeneager Miss Fine might have been, the one we *all* could have been, if only the world had been kinder.

Another thing Miss Fine and I have in common: We're both teachers, though most of my students are college freshmen. I think about my students when I watch *Booksmart*, especially the girls. I wonder, when they watch, do they see themselves in Molly and Amy, or is the insecure Miss Fine at the party as familiar to them as it is to me? Is the world today *that* different for young women?

I hope my students see themselves in Molly and Amy. I hope things are different. But if they don't, and if things aren't, I'm glad *Booksmart* exists. I'm glad Molly and Amy show teenage girls the smart *and* fun *and* multidimensional young women they all deserve to be.

YOU MUST ALWAYS HAVE FAITH IN YOURSELF - *LEGALLY BLONDE*, AND MY MOMMY, AND ME

Elizabeth Teets

My mother is a blonde. I mean this literally, but also figuratively and spiritually. She is a blonde in every sense of the word. She has the most fun, has the blonde ambition, is remembered by everyone she meets, and above all…is a total knockout.

A few years back we visited my great-grandmother who by that point had Alzheimer's so advanced she didn't remember who my grandma, her daughter, was anymore. But she instantly recognized my mom, Rebecca, when she walked in the room. She recognized "Becky" because Becky is blonde.

My mom has the other things that we associate with blondes, stunning blue eyes, perfectly white teeth, and a shoe collection that rivals the paintings at the Louvre. Having her as a mother creates a world of calm because I know that everything will always turn out fine when it is in her extremely capable, perfectly manicured hands.

That all being said, my mother does not consider herself a girly girl. Although she does have an unhealthy amount of MAC cosmetics points and countless skincare products thanks to her FitFabFun subscription. She loves sports, is inhumanly strong for her 5"3 frame, and would prefer to change her own oil in her car, but she simply does not have the time anymore.

That's another thing about my mom, she is always busy. Too busy. Busy working, busy raising me, busy doing whatever blondes do. Giving us everything.

She is certainly too busy to go to the movies, my favorite thing. There is nothing my brunette head loves more than taking in two hours of cinema in a dark room. But my blonde mom does not have time for that, and she would also require a more comfortable chair and prefers to not risk getting sticky, so she watches movies at home.

Legally Blonde was the first movie I saw my mother truly love. This was not to say she didn't love other movies - there were many she did. Growing up, my mother had a small collection of VHS tapes she loved that she would let me watch regularly. But none of them compared for how much she seemed to love *Legally Blonde*.

Despite her very refined palette for cinema, I don't think she ever considered film an interest of hers. And although she may not have realized it, my mother had curated in our living room a sophisticated collection of the finest 90s and early aughts cult classics. We had copies of *Mermaids*, *She's All That*, *A Very Brady Sequel*, and *Tommy Boy*. But *Legally Blonde*, oh she loved that movie.

At ten years old, I took notice of how Reese Witherspoon as Elle Woods, *Legally Blonde*'s perky sorority girl, made my mother laugh. I love anything that makes my mother laugh. After seeing my mother latch onto a piece of candy pink cinema filled with outfits, I too became obsessed with the film. As a future comedian, I paid attention to anything that made my favorite person laugh.

I also love *Legally Blonde* - it is undoubtedly my favorite movie. I know every line, every outfit, and every major decision I have ever made in my life has been while driving in my 2006 Kia Optima while listening to the absolute banger of a soundtrack. Elle Woods is the best character within modern cinema. She is layered, complicated, fabulously styled, unable to be bamboozled and full of grit. I was lucky enough to grow up with my own Elle Woods, my mom. Like Elle, she was an incredibly economically mobile, driven, beautiful and, of course, impeccably dressed woman who still to this day does not consider herself a girly girl or a knockout of which she is both.

If you are unfamiliar with *Legally Blonde*, you should put down this book and correct yourself immediately. But for the truly pop culture deprived, *Legally Blonde* stars Reese Witherspoon as Elle Woods, a blonde, pink wearing, Bel-Air sorority girl with a tiny dog in her purse. A sort of Paris Hilton-Britney Spears-Cameron Diaz hybrid, she is every early 00s stereotype rolled into one. A masterclass in performing early 2000s femininity.

At our hero's beginning, Elle is getting a degree in fashion and merchandising while attending a fake college they made up for the movie which is supposed to be UCLA. Elle is looking forward to a dinner with her boyfriend Warner Huntington III, a dinner where she assumes he will propose and she will start her life as a Beverly Hills trophy wife.

In preparation for this date, accompanied by her sorority sisters, she goes to pick out the perfect outfit. While deciding between blue sequins or staying safe in her signature color, a sly sales woman attempts to pull a fast one on Elle. Assuming she is just "a dumb blonde with daddy's credit card," the sales woman presents Elle with a clearance gown hoping to sell it at full price and take the commission.

At first Elle seems interested, but this isn't just another dumb blonde. This is Elle Woods. Elle asks the sales woman if it's "half-loop stitch-on low-viscosity rayon."

When the sales woman continues the charade, Elle shows us that she is a fashion expert and unable to be hoodwinked.

"It's impossible to do a half loop stitch on china silk, it would snag the fabric."

She was aware the dress was old. Up on every trend, she saw it in the June *Vogue* a year ago.

"If you were trying to sell it to me at full price, you picked the wrong girl."

Sure, she is another blonde, but not a dumb one. She's Elle Woods.

Like Elle, my mom always manages to stun people as they underestimate her with grace and panache. You should see her at a car dealership. The woman is unsinkable.

Later that day, Elle is once again underestimated but this time by her boyfriend Warner. Arriving at dinner for what she expects to be the most important dinner of her life, to her dismay, she is instead dumped.

Warner claims that in order to fulfill his family's expectations (becoming a senator by the time he's thirty) he needs "a Jackie not a Marilyn." Leading Elle to utter the perfect line: "So you are breaking up with me because I'm too...blonde!"

At my mother's beginning, or at least the beginning as it

concerns me, her daughter who watched her every move, she was a single mom who had me at nineteen. This meant as a child I got to see her early twenties, her own Elle Woods years. Although she was never a member of a sorority with a tiny dog, I can't imagine people talked to her that differently. Aren't all stereotypes we put onto women pretty much the same?

I remember even then that many people did not see my mom as serious. An adult yes, but not the same as my teacher or my grandma. She was something else entirely.

After Warner dumps Elle, she spirals into a depression she has never known. At this point Elle has never felt a rejection. Sorority president and former homecoming queen, no one had ever found Elle anything other than perfect. Instead of wallowing in this pity Elle takes action. Suddenly realizing her path to seriousness and hopefully back to Warner's heart: Law School.

Elle heads straight to her university guidance counselor's office and expresses her desire to attend Harvard Law School and win the love of her life back. The guidance counselor asks if she has back-ups. Elle doesn't have any - she's going to Harvard.

My mother, also a firm believer in education and the doors it opened, also saw her path in the form of higher education. She worked endlessly to complete her degree all while working full-time and taking care of me. I had received the unique education in real time of watching my mother live her American Dream. My mom is now an executive, which is not a lawyer but is close enough and requires the same wardrobe. She's a boss and is awesome. My mom never has back-up plans. She has plan A and plan A will work out.

Always.

Naturally, Elle gets into Harvard Law School. Something that shocks Warner when he sees her on campus. Uttering Elle to ask the question: "What, like it's hard?" A sentence that could also sum up my mother's entire personality. Never let them see you sweat.

A fish out of water, Elle has a hard time at Harvard. Everyone around her is wearing neutral colors and no one wants to help her plan a great mixer. I am sure my mother felt similarly in her early twenties - no one else had a kid.

On her first day at Harvard, Elle introduces herself and her dog Bruiser, as Gemini vegetarians. My mom is also a Gemini, although I don't think she could ever be a vegetarian.

Since we didn't attend Harvard, at the time we were living in a Corvallis, Oregon trailer park. That being said, my mother does not appreciate that I set the scene as "Interior: Trailer Park" in my writing and she would like me to inform you all that she was in her early twenties, a single parent, and a homeowner which is impressive. And also to not imply any "wrong side of the tracks" vibes in my books, as it was quote, "for a very short period of time and misleading to say that."

It is a very Elle Woods thing to inform you of this truth.

In *Legally Blonde*, Elle poses as her friend Paulette's (Jennifer Coolidge) attorney to help her get her dog back from her ex who also took the mobile home they had both shared. Throughout the film Paulette refers to the mobile home as a trailer, Elle Woods refers to it as a residence.

Anyways, in our Corvallis, Oregon residence, my mom finished her college degree and graduated from a private university.

I'm not trying to ruin the movie for you and there is a pretty important court case that happens so you should still watch it but, despite her struggles, Elle Woods gets the hang of Harvard, refuses to take Warner back, and graduates top of her class and gives the commencement speech. I watched my mother graduate from college, the same year the film was released. They wore the same black graduation robes.

I asked my mom recently why she loved *Legally Blonde* so much. We bought *Legally Blonde 2: Red White and Blonde* in its iconic baby pink DVD case on the day it came out without even seeing it, that's how much she loved the first one. At first she mused on our shared love of Reese Witherspoon. In the Teets household, we stan Reese. My mom loved *Cruel Intentions*. I have always preferred *Freeway*, because it's number one on John Waters's list of movies that will corrupt you and kinda scary.

My mom also said she loved how much of a smart ditz Elle was. But when I dug deeper, Rebecca paused and gave me her answer, "It could have been a regular stereotypical love story, but she was like screw you, become her own person."

My mother embodies many of Elle Woods's traits. She would help a friend get her dog back, it would not surprise me if she could get into Harvard. She would never reveal a secret told to her in confidence by a friend, she loves fashion. She is blonde and definitely her own person.

Growing up I got a front row seat to the story of Rebecca, my own blonde Gemini. I never saw her falter when things got hard, I rarely saw her stumble and even when she did she got back up again and showed the world how valuable she could be. I am also positive that we attended at least one birthday party for a dog around 2001.

To me Elle's story is about bending over backwards to make a man love you, only to fall in love with yourself.

Legally Blonde is my comfort movie, I love watching Elle go through every challenge with grace and humor. I love her restlessness, optimism, and effortless social grace. I often have the movie on as I putter around my apartment and every time it makes me happy. Blondes can put people at ease. They make everything seem less serious, even when it is. I choose to see that as a strength.

Elle Woods is my ultimate character, the best leading lady in all of cinema. I like this fictional character so much I have a clock I bought off Etsy that says, "do it for her" with many tiny pictures of Elle at Harvard. I have it to remind myself of Elle's graduation speech:

"Most importantly you must always have faith in yourself."

When I look at it, I know I can overcome whatever I am going through just like Elle overcame Warner and people saying orange was the new pink. I put on "Perfect Day" by Hoku and handle my shit.

Maybe it's for Elle. Maybe it's for her, my mom, the blonde.

AFTERWORD

Anthony Hudson

Out of all our programming at the Hollywood Theatre, nobody complains about any series as much as they do than at *Isn't She Great*. After I took my job programming there, Teets approached me with her idea: let's show comedies starring hilarious women and each edition will open with stand-up from an also-hilarious woman. Yes, perfect. Done. But nothing is as contentious as women, it seems, and especially women who have the gall to tell jokes.

I was still new and fresh at my job when I pitched this series and no, I had no idea what I was doing. Wait—am I *not* supposed to send an organization-wide email to everyone when I want to propose new programming? I was so proud when I wrote what I thought was an irrefutable feminist pitch for a series launching with a screening of *Romy and Michele's High School Reunion* and hit send to the entire office mailing list. *They will love this*, I thought, *everyone will love this and everyone will love me. Look at the good I do.*

Thus arrived our first spate of complaints. For one thing, I was not supposed to send an organization-wide email to everyone detailing a series pitch, however feminist and irrefutable I thought it might be. Second, sorry girl, it turns out what you want to do is not feminist: Teets and I wanted to call the series *Atta Girl* in honor of Margaret, the drunk secretary—I'm sorry, drunk administrative assistant, no, sorry, drunk office queen—in *9 to 5*, the one played by Peggy Pope

109

who mutters "atta girl" each time a declaration of self-care is made or a high-heeled foot is put down.

"*Atta Girl* is infantilizing," we were told. "It's not just infantilizing, it's dehumanizing."

We cited our source material. "*Atta Girl* is a deep-cut homage to an anticorporate queen who champions agency in a classic feminist office comedy masterpiece," we explained. "Haven't you seen *9 to 5*?"

"OK," we heard back, "but also it kinda sounds like dog food?"

Not wanting to dehumanize women with our feminist comedy series, but perhaps not also wanting to be confused with dog food as Portlanders scan weeklies for movie listings, we decided to scrap *Atta Girl*, despite it being our best and favorite name. We would have to save knowing winks at the audience for when we were on stage. Best to be more straightforward in print—but with what title?

Queens of Comedy? Taken.

Laughing Ladies? Kill me.

#YesMyGhostbusters? Don't want to court men's rights activists.

Women Are Funny? Too political.

"What about…" I scraped the interior of my brain in my thoughts.

"Let's go with *Isn't She Great*," Teets said.

"Like the Bette Midler movie, the one with her and Nathan Lane in which she plays Jacqueline Susann, author of *Valley of the Dolls*, and I never saw it but I was always confused why something so niche was always in the five dollar bin at

Wal-Mart back home as a teenager?" I asked.

"Yes," Teets said. "But also it's something people say when they like a woman comic. 'Isn't she great,' they'll say."

"That's so safe," I said.

"Our best alternative hates women," Teets said.

"But loves dog food!" I said.

"*Isn't She Great*, it is," Teets declared.

A month later, Isn't She Great launched with our sold-out screening of *Romy and Michele's High School Reunion*. We were triumphant. The audience was captivated by the previously unheard-of experience of laughing both before and during a movie. If we had started doing this years in the future when Trump wasn't president, we might have even said "we did it, Joe," to each other in congratulatory celebration.

And then a new slate of complaints came in.

"Some people were concerned that anti-male jokes were made before the screening," we were told.

"I'm sorry?" we asked, bewildered. This was the last thing we expected to hear.

"There are concerns that your feminist comedy show hates men."

But it does, we thought, while simultaneously saying the opposite out loud. We opened that first screening with a few jokes about how women are hilarious—or "hysterically funny," in a play on the sexist idea of *hysteria*—and it turns out men just aren't. They'd had their time. Move over, fellas. Now we had been informed that our series—in which we, again, show funny movies starring funny women, and open with funny women on a microphone—not only hated women, it hated men too. Who's safe from *Isn't She Great*?

I mostly laughed off the concerns of anti-male sentiment with our staff while noting that we would be sure to amply warn attendees at the top of each show that stand-up comedy featuring opinions, ideas, and punchlines would be in store for them and that they could temporarily leave the auditorium or browse on their phone if they wanted to only enjoy the pre-approved laughs they'd come to expect from our programmed films. We pushed ever onward.

At the next screening—another sold-out presentation, this time of *Troop Beverly Hills* starring Shelley Long—Teets and I even warned the comic, Ella Gale, to skew toward safer material to make up for what was an alarming number of children in the audience. Ella did. And yet after that screening, even more complaints came flooding in.

"It's inappropriate for a young lady to talk about such things," we were told by a senior audience member, and in this case, "such things" referred to dating. Like the film itself, all material was PG. Of course, that's PG by 1980s standards, before PG-13 was implemented, but still!

To offer some comparative background, I have screened movies at the Hollywood since 2015. At my best-known show, *Queer Horror*—the only LGBTQ horror screening series in the country—where I first met Teets, we get away with everything but murder in our drag preshow sketches and deliver them to a consistently sold-out audience. Such content has included:

- Setting Donald Trump on fire;
- Blowing up Mitch McConnell, Paul Ryan, and Donald Trump;
- Fighting a giant, tentacled prolapse belonging to

Donald Trump, and then setting it on fire, all while dressed as Cher;

- JK Rowling getting stabbed to death by Toonces, the cat who could drive a car;

- Exposed breasts in a burlesque act, not to mention a fully exposed ass—and maybe a little more—when an all-but-naked man in a jockstrap was sacrificed by witches onstage with his ass in the air, a pose he would be in for the remainder of the show;

- Uttering words like "bitch," "cunt," "limp-dicked twats," and "TERF cucks," as well as successfully coining the term "clussy" on stage in 2016, to the benefit of the Internet;

- Me, armed with a newly christened vape pen and post-2016 election depression, rambling at the audience for 47 minutes straight while introducing a short film program

Despite all this and to the best of my knowledge, we've never had one complaint lodged against us at *Queer Horror*. *The Portland Mercury* called us "a goddamn Portland treasure." The show has become so popular that parents even bring their kids, perhaps just to see the horrified look on my face when I, dressed as Annabelle the haunted doll, make eye contact with particularly judgemental little girls as I spew profanity into my microphone through a terrible Scottish accent.

In other words, we can get away with anything at *Queer Horror*—where men dress as women, women dress as men, and genders of all varieties dress as dolls, mermaids, witches, and pop culture caricatures—and yet the very simple act of having a woman recite comedy on a microphone in the exact same venue is too big an ask. It turns out heightened, made-up versions of women, covered in glitter and fake eyelashes, the kind resembling Dolly Parton but covered in blood and wreaking destruction—am I just describing Gwen Shamblin?—are hilarious, but to see the real deal, whether cis or trans, telling jokes in an everyday look is just as offensive as a woman seeking healthcare.

Now Teets and I open *Isn't She Great* screenings with this:

"Thank you for coming to *Isn't She Great*, where we celebrate hysterically funny women in comedy. As a heads-up, there is stand-up comedy before the movie tonight, but don't worry—we already went ahead and complained to the management for you."

That one always gets a laugh. And yet, even still, even after, we hear:

"Women shouldn't talk like that."

"Her language is unacceptable."

"Men might feel uncomfortable."

"Nobody wants to see stand-up comedy before a movie, let alone stand-up comedy at all."

Teets and I tend to agree with this final sentiment: the two of us, as a drag performer and a stand-up comic respectively, hate our professions.

Luckily, through all this, every complaint we get at every film we screen only stokes the giddy flames of our antipatriarchal (not necessarily to be confused with anti-male) mission. After each screening we run to the house manager to get the dirty details: *tell us what they said this time! Who did we offend? How are women, not religions or politicians or corporations, destroying the fabric of society today?* Now we collect each complaint like trophies, like two Millennial feminist Predators—as in the dreadlocked sci-fi monster, not Asia Argento—fancified with skulls dangling from our bandoliers. These are our kills.

And with each complaint—each ongoing, individual acknowledgment that a funny woman can push people past the brink and completely ruin their days—it's like Peggy Pope, as perfect, drunk Margaret in *9 to 5*, who died in 2020 at the ripe age of 91, and who we would have memorialized with a screening that year were it not for COVID, is smiling back at us with approval as she tosses another office file in the trash.

Atta girl.

ABOUT THE CONTRIBUTORS

MEGAN J. KALEITA is an essayist and memoirist living in the PAC Northwest. Her debut essay collection, *This Book is Brought to You By My Student Loans* is available through Clash Books. Her work has appeared in Ravishly, Hello Horror, Daily Drunk Mag, Luna Station Quarterly, and Lady Spike. Do not ask her for coffee. She won't get it for you.

SAMANTHA MANN is a Brooklyn based essayist. She is the author of *Putting Out: Essays on Otherness*. She edited the anthology, *I Feel Love: Notes on Queer Joy*.

ANDRIA KENNEDY works her sense of humor into everything - except sleeping outdoors (there's no compromise there). Her essays have appeared in *Chicken Soup for the Soul: My Clever, Curious, Caring Cat* and *Lessons Learned From My Cat*, The Strategist, Open Minds Quarterly, Electric Lit, The Doe, Points in Case, and HuffPost Personal. When she isn't writing, she's invariably fighting with her cat (demon) for the comfiest throws in the house. Oh, and spending time with her husband, three other cats, and greyhound in front of the television with a pop culture favorite.

AUBREY JACOBOWITZ is an actor, comedian, and writer from Los Angeles. They've produced successful indie comedy shows in Los Angeles and San Francisco, toured and performed nationally at festivals such as Crom Comedy

Festival in Denver, and were written up by Time Out as a powerhouse talent. They can be found collaging on the fourth of July or smoking under a full moon.

TOJU ADELAJA is a Nigerian-British writer and chick-flick connoisseur. Her work has appeared in publications such as Glamour U.K. and Black Ballad.

ELLA GALE is a writer, director, and comedian in Los Angeles. Her work has appeared in McSweeney's, Reductress, and the Hard Times.

MICHELE THEIL is a journalist focusing on culture, race, LGBT+ issues and investigative pieces. She has been published in VICE, Insider, Glamour, and others. She watches all the *Bring It On* movies at least once a year.

YAËL KRINSKY is writer and comedian based in Boston, where she works in TV and Film Production. She holds a writing and performance degree from Bard College. She currently lives with her dog Midge.

LANA SCHWARTZ is a writer who was born and raised in New York City, where she continues to live today. Her work has been published on The New Yorker, McSweeney's, Shondaland, Glamour, InStyle, and more. Her book "Build Your Own Romantic Comedy" was released by Ulysses Press in March 2020. For more about Lana - as well as instructions on how to pronounce her name - visit www.lanalikebanana.com.

MEG WALTERS is a Canadian-British writer currently living in London. Her writing has appeared in GQ, The Daily Beast, Vulture, Cosmopolitan, Glamour and others. She is a great lover of classic films, rom-coms, period dramas, pop culture, books and style and tries to write about them all as often as possible. Find her on Twitter @wordsbymeg

ANNA SIMS is a writer and professor with work in *Electric Literature*, *Dame*, *Shondaland*, and *The Millions*.

ANTHONY HUDSON (Confederated Tribes of Grand Ronde, Siletz) is an artist and writer also known as Portland's premier drag clown Carla Rossi. Anthony's performance work, from his award-winning solo show *Looking for Tiger Lily* to *Queer Horror*, the only LGBTQ horror film and performance series in the country, have earned him national fellowships, international engagements, and sainthood from the Portland Sisters of Perpetual Indulgence. A 2023 FSG Writer's Fellowship finalist, Anthony's writing has appeared in American Theatre and Arts and International Affairs, and he is currently adapting *Looking for Tiger Lily* into a book.

ABOUT THE EDITOR

Elizabeth Teets is an Oregon born writer, comedian, screenwriter, and fashionista. Her work has appeared in Los Angeles Times, New York Times, Repeller, Catapult, Reductress, and more. She lives in Los Angeles where she is waiting for her group chat to respond.

Find Elizabeth online at:
elizabethteets.com
instagram.com/elteets

ACKNOWLEDGMENTS

This book would not be possible without my mother and her excellent taste in VHS tapes she kept inside our home. I love you so much mommy. Remember when I was trying to tell you about this book and you were convinced I was telling you I was pregnant?

I am indebted to my friends and fellow artists who encouraged me during this process including Caroline Shannon, Chloe Caldwell, Anna Valenzuela, and Danielle Neublock.

I would like to thank my entire chosen family but especially Julie Spilker, Trevor Harvey, and Pepper Pepper for their love, support, and many zooms and phone calls.

Thanks to the weird start-up job that laid me off after I started editing this anthology and especially thanks to UNEMPLOYMENT BENEFITS.

Enormous thanks to my writing group Lana Schwarts and Leigh Castro. I promise I will have a better celebrity sighting next week.

To Samantha Mann for making editing an anthology look like the coolest thing a girl can do, and for sending my pitch.

Samantha Atzeni! Thank you for agreeing to publish this anthology and answering all my insane emails. I love our phone calls and will keep writing books to keep talking to you.

To all the writers who contributed! Thank you for all your work and especially your stories and support! We did it!

I would like to thank tall handsome Brandon for agreeing to escort me to all my readings in the foreseeable future, your broad shoulders and perfect teeth will certainly double my sales. If you are a man wondering why you have a copy of this anthology you probably wanted to talk to Brandon.

Enormous shout out to COLD BREW and popcorn as dinner.

The real ones. Thanks to my friends of all sorts Kevin Blumeyer, Amanda Clem, Red O'Hare and Stuart Thompson.

I would also like to Tomy Bach who I know is still with me.

This anthology would also not be possible without The Hollywood Theatre but especially Connor, Matt, Sean, Jamie, and that ghost who lives in the upper right theater that just watches people watch movies.

Thanks to four dollar sweat shorts I edited most of these essays in, one day you will pair with a glamorous floral silk robe but you're amazing just as you are.

To my cat Weetzie who was not helpful when sitting on my computer but is still the best. Thanks for not running away and choosing to spend your life with me of all people.

To John Waters for teaching me everything I need to know about being an artist, queer, and person.

Grammy, thanks for teaching me how to be funny.

And I would especially like to express my enormous gratitude to everyone who worked on all the films mentioned in this anthology. Thank you for making the movie magic that shaped so many futures.

To all women who dare to be funny and to the enormously talented comedic actresses who made the characters in these movies real.

Anthony, my final girl, arch rival, and soul mate. I love you so much thanks for creating so much with me.

To Elle Woods. Do it for her.

BIBLIOGRAPHY

The creative works referenced and cited in this collection are copyrighted to their respective owners and used within the guidelines of fair use. The films and one television episode listed below are cited within the collection and referenced to continue the cultural conversation relating to the work.

Ephron, Nora. *Sleepless in Seattle. Screenplay* by Nora Ephron, David S. Ward, and Jeff Arch. TriStar Pictures, 1993.

Ephron, Nora. *You've Got Mail.* Screenplay by Nora Ephron and Delia Ephron. Lauren Shuler Donner Productions, 1998.

Frankel, David, director. *The Devil Wears Prada.* Screenplay by Aline Brosh McKenna. Fox 2000 Pictures, Wendy Finerman Productions, Dune Entertainment, 2006.

Herek, Stephen, director. *Don't Tell Mom the Babysitter's Dead.* Screenplay by Neil Landau and Tara Ison. HBO, Outlaw Productions, and Cinema Plus L.P., 1991.

Kanew, Jeff, director. *Troop Beverly Hills.* Screenplay by Pamela Norris and Margaret Grieco Oberman. Weintraub Entertainment Group and Fries Entertainment, 1989.

Luketic, Robert, director. *Legally Blonde.* Screenplay by Karen McCullah Lutz and Kirsten Smith. MGM and Marc Platt Productions, 2001.

Maguire, Sharon, director. *Bridget Jones's Diary.* Screenplay by

Richard Curtis, Andrew Davies, and Helen Fielding. Universal Pictures, Little Bird, StudioCanal, and Working Title Films, 2001.

McCulloch, Bruce, director. *Superstar*. Screenplay by Steve Koren. SNL Studios, 1999.

Ortega, Kenny, director. *Hocus Pocus*. Screenplay by Mick Garris and Neil Cuthbert. Walt Disney Pictures, 1993.

Payne, Alexander, director. *Election*. Screenplay by Alexander Payne and Jim Taylor. MTV Productions and Bona Fide Productions, 1999.

Petrie, Donald, director. *Miss Congeniality*. Screenplay by Marc Lawrence, Katie Ford, and Caryn Lucas. Fortis Films, NPV Entertainment, Castle Rock Entertainment, and Village Roadshow Pictures, 2000.

Reed, Peyton, director. *Bring It On*. Screenplay by Jessica Bendinger. Beacon Pictures, 2000.

Reiner, Rob. *When Harry Met Sally...* Screenplay by Nora Ephron. Castle Rock Entertainment and Nelson Entertainment, 1989.

Roeg, Nicolas, director. *The Witches*. Screenplay by Allan Scott. Lorimar Film Entertainment and Jim Henson Productions, 1990.

Stein, Darren, director. *Jawbreaker*. Screenplay by Darren Stein. TriStar Pictures, Kramer-Tornell Productions, and Crossroads Films, 1996.

Weiner, Matthew, writer. *Mad Men*. Season 1, episode 1, "Smoke Gets in Your Eyes." Directed by Alan Taylor, featuring Jon Hamm, Elisabeth Moss, Vincent Kartheiser, and Christina Hendricks. Aired July 19, 2007 in broadcast syndication. AMC Original Productions.

Wilde, Olivia, director. *Booksmart*. Screenplay by Emily Halpern, Sarah Haskins, Susanna Fogel, and Katie Silberman. Annapurna Pictures and Gloria Sanchez Productions, 2019.

Wilson, Hugh, director. *The First Wives Club*. Screenplay by Robert Harling. Paramount Pictures, 1996.

A Note to our Furious Readers

From all of us at Read Furiously, we hope you enjoyed our latest title, *Isn't She Great: Writers on Women-Led Comedies From* 9 to 5 *to* Booksmart.

At Read Furiously, we wish to add an active voice to the world we all share by nurturing positive change in our local and global communities. It is with this in mind that we pledge to donate a portion of these book sales to causes that are special to Read Furiously. These causes are chosen with the intent to better the lives of others who are struggling to tell their own stories.

The causes we support encourage a sense of social responsibility associated with the act of reading. Each cause has been researched thoroughly, discussed openly, and voted upon carefully by Read Furiously editors.

To find out more about who, what, why, and where Read Furiously lends its support, please visit our website at readfuriously.com/charity

Happy reading and giving, Furious Readers!

Read Often, Read Well,
Read Furiously!

Look for these other great titles from

Read Furiously

Read Often. Read Well.

The One 'n Done Series

What About Tuesday

Girls, They'll Never Take Us Alive

Brethren Hollow

Helium

The Legend of Dave Bradley

The Path Home

Showboi / Too Deep Too Care

Wind to Space (April 2024)

W(h)ine and Cheese (July 2024)

Brookly Family Album (September 2024)

Fiction

Working Through This

Chasing Harmony

Urban Folk Tales: Stories

Parade of Streetlights (June 2023)

Americana: Stories (July 2023)

Poetry

Until the roof lifted off

Whatever You Thought, Think Again

Dear Terror

Silk City Sparrow

All These Little Stars

Anthologies

The World Takes: Life in the Garden State

Stay Salty: Life in the Garden State

Furious Lit: Tell Me A Story

Graphic Novels

The MOTHER Principle

Brian & Bobbi

In the Fallout

Pursuit: A Collection of Artwork

Northwood Meadows: Lifestyle

First

Northwood Meadows: Moments (May, 202

Last of the Pops (July 2024)

Non-Fiction

Putting Out: Essays on Otherness

We don't do "just okay" anymore

Nerd Traveler

I Feel Love: Notes on Queer Joy

Isn't She Great: Writers on Women Led

Comedies from 9 to 5 to Booksmart

Children's Books

The Little Gray Witch

The Little Boy Who Wasn't A Witch

Printed in the USA
CPSIA information can be obtained
at www.ICGtesting.com
LVHW010731070124
767854LV00007B/14